EduRishi Eduventures Pvt. Ltd.
Handcrafted EdTech of Bharat

EduRishi's S.T.E.A.M. Tales Part-2

Author - Dr. Jitesh Jain

Copyright © 2024 EduRishi Eduventures Pvt. Ltd.

All Rights Reserved.

EduRishi Eduventures Pvt. Ltd.

Sr. No. 54/A/1, Dattawadi Nere, Tal-Mulshi,

near Hinjawdi, Pune, India, Maharashtra.

Pin-411033

www.edurishi.in

Printed in India

Preface

Welcome to the enthralling universe of EduRishi, where the boundaries of learning are surpassed, and imagination reigns supreme. We are delighted to introduce our latest creation: a captivating flipbook chronicling the adventures of Alien Talos from Onidura as he embarks on an extraordinary quest for science on Earth.

Within the pages of this flipbook, you will delve into a narrative infused with Science, Technology, Engineering, Arts, and Mathematics (STEAM), as Talos navigates through thrilling challenges and discoveries. Each chapter is meticulously crafted to not only entertain but also to ignite curiosity and foster a love for learning.

Inspired by the visionary National Education Policy (NEP) 2020, our storytelling approach is designed to empower learners of all ages and backgrounds. From unravelling the mysteries of the universe alongside Alien Talos to fostering creativity and problem-solving skills, EduRishi's Story-based STEAM Quest Flipbook promises an enriching experience for all.

As you embark on this adventure, you will witness first-hand the transformative power of storytelling in education, guided by EduRishi's dedication to excellence and innovation. Whether you're a young explorer thirsting for knowledge, an educator seeking to inspire imagination, or a lifelong learner on a quest for discovery, we invite you to join us on this exhilarating journey.

Thank you for joining us as we embark on this extraordinary quest for scientific enlightenment.

Warm regards,

Dr. Jitesh Jain

Co-Founder & CEO

EduRishi Eduventures Pvt. Ltd.

India's First E-learning Platform

Based on the Implications of National Education Policy 2020.

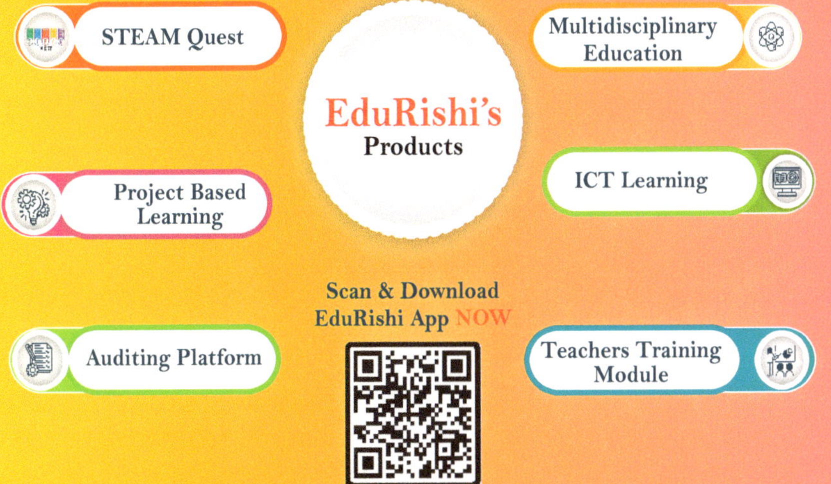

EduRishi: Revolutionizing Education with India's National Education Policy 2020

EduRishi is India's pioneering e-learning platform dedicated to implementing the National Education Policy 2020. Our innovative platform offers a comprehensive range of educational resources and tools designed to empower students, teachers and Schools alike. From interactive lessons and personalized learning pathways to collaborative teaching modules, EduRishi is reshaping the educational landscape by fostering a culture of holistic learning and skill development. Join us in shaping the future of education in India with EduRishi.

STORY SO FAR

EDURISHI
STORY SO FAR
From the planet Onidura, an extraterrestrial named Talos has descended to Earth in quest of life. Where he studied about the kingdom Plantae and Anamalia with his mate, Anahita, the water lily plant.
Talos encountered a group of students and expressed curiosity about the human respiratory system. Taking the lead, Sophie stepped forward enthusiastically to enlighten Talos about the intricacies of the respiratory system, capturing his attention with her knowledge and confidence.
Natural Fabrics
Wool
Cotton
Synthetic Fabrics
Talos delves into diverse professions, seeking knowledge on their mechanisms for a better understanding of human livelihood. He explores the sources of energy employed across various occupations, broadening his awareness to enhance his comprehension of the intricate web of human activities.
With Onidura planet destroyed, Talos embarks on a journey through the solar system in search of a new home. Filled with determination, he meticulously assesses planets, weighing factors like distance and suitability, as he devotes himself to finding a replacement for the Onidura.
Coal
Oil
Gas

While exploring Earth, Talos becomes engrossed, forgetting his mission. In response, the King of Onidura prepares for an attack to make Earth their new home. Before launching the assault, they harness various forms of energy for the impending conquest.

His friends enlighten him about the disasters and diseases they face on Earth, concluding that no planet is entirely safe. Motivated to address these challenges, Talos learns about various diseases, their variants, and methods for treatment.

ZORG – WE ARE PREPARED AND READY TO ATTACK.

TALOS - BUT MASTER I HAVE NOT COMPLETED MY
          MISSION YET AS THERE IS A LOT MORE TO LEARN
          ABOUT EARTH.

ZORG –   NO WE DON'T HAVE MUCH TIME. ONIDURA IS
          DEGRADING FAST ANd WE CAN'T WASTE TIME
          ANYMORE. WE ARE TAKING OFF SOON AND
          WILL CONTACT YOU ONCE WE ARE NEAR THE
          EARTH'S ATMOSPHERE.

1

I just received a message from Onidura General Zorg is ready to attack Earth.
I have a plan. The next time he contacts you tell him to land at the farm nearby. We will all go there with you.
You will have to convince him not to attack us and leave our planet alone.
But how?
2

ZORG – WE HAVE ENTERED INTO THE EARTH'S ATMOSPHERE GIVE US THE COORDINATES TO LAND.

TALOS – MASTER, I REQUEST YOU TO ABANDON THE MISSION.

ZORG – FOOL, DON'T WASTE TIME. SEND ME THE COORDINATES.

TALOS – OK MASTER, I HAVE SENT THE COORDNATES TO MASTER PILOT.

3

TALOS, SOPHIE AND HER FRIENDS ARRIVE AT THE NEARBY FARM WHERE ZORG'S SPACESHIP WAS LANDING.
Who are these people with you? I sent you to collect information not to make friends on Earth.
Welcome General Zorg.
Master, they are inhabitants of the Earth who have helped me in understanding the life on Earth.
But why have they come here?
4

Mr Zorg, I am Sophie and we know all about your planet your mission to colonize earth. But we the people of Earth request you to not do that.
But why should I change my mind? Our planet is degrading and we need a home soon.
This is why we have brought you here. We wanted to show you how to build life on your own planet or some other vacant planet like we have build our Earth.
5

EDURISHI
This is my family's farmland. This is where we grow our food. Like your planet there are many but today we have progressed so much that we have plenty of food from various sources and we know many new methods to grow food.
Food is essential for all living organisms. Plants store it in organs like fruits, tubers, and seeds. Animals and humans rely on this stored food, with larger animals relying on smaller ones.
6
Scan for Food Types Video
From Animal
From Plants
Plant food products include vegetables, fruits, cereals, pulses, spices, nuts, and oils, primarily sourced from green plants.
Animal food products include meat, poultry, fish, eggs, dairy products (like milk, cheese, and yogurt), honey, and insects, primarily sourced from animals.
7
5

Master, I have met different organisms here. Every species is different from each other. But they all are interdependent on each other.
We eat differently because Earth is not just one place. It is divided on many continents and countries. Every part of the Earth is different and has different food culture.
Carnivores feed on other animals while the Herbivores feed on plants and there are Omnivores too who feed on both plants and animals.
But we Onidurans are all equal. We all eat the same.
8
Like organisms the food we eat is also different. Every type of food has its own benefit.
Master I have learnt that the food on earth is very nutritious and capable of providing energy.
But I don't see any food here all I see is large green fields.
Mr Zorg, let me invite you to my house so I can show you how food on Earth looks like.
9
6

NAME OF VITAMINS AND MINERALS	DEFICIENCY DISEASE OR DISORDER	MAIN SYMPTOMS
Vitamin A	Night blindness	Poor or loss of vision in darkness (night), sometimes complete loss of vision.
Vitamin B1	Beriberi	Weak muscles, and very little energy to work.
Vitamin C	Scurvy	Bleeding gums.
Vitamin D	Rickets	Bones become soft and bent.
Calcium	Hypocalcemia	Weak bones, tooth decay.
Iodine	Goitre	Glands in the neck appear swollen, mental disability in children
Iron	Anaemia	Weakness

11

So you just grow food in you farms and eat. It looks so simple.
No Mr Zorg it is not that simple only the pure food can give us benefits of nutrition and energy. Impure foods instead make us sick.
We must clean food to remove impure, undesirable, unwanted and harmful components and to obtain pure and useful components.
Pure substances are elements and compounds Impure Substances are those that have multiple types of component particles.
EDURISHI
Master, I told you about different states of matter on Earth. Like food every matter on earth can be pure or impure.
12
The cleaning process of a farm to obtain grains involves several steps to remove impurities and unwanted materials. These steps include.
Harvesting
Threshing
This is the barn where we keep our farm produce.
Handpicking
Winnowing
Sieving
13
8

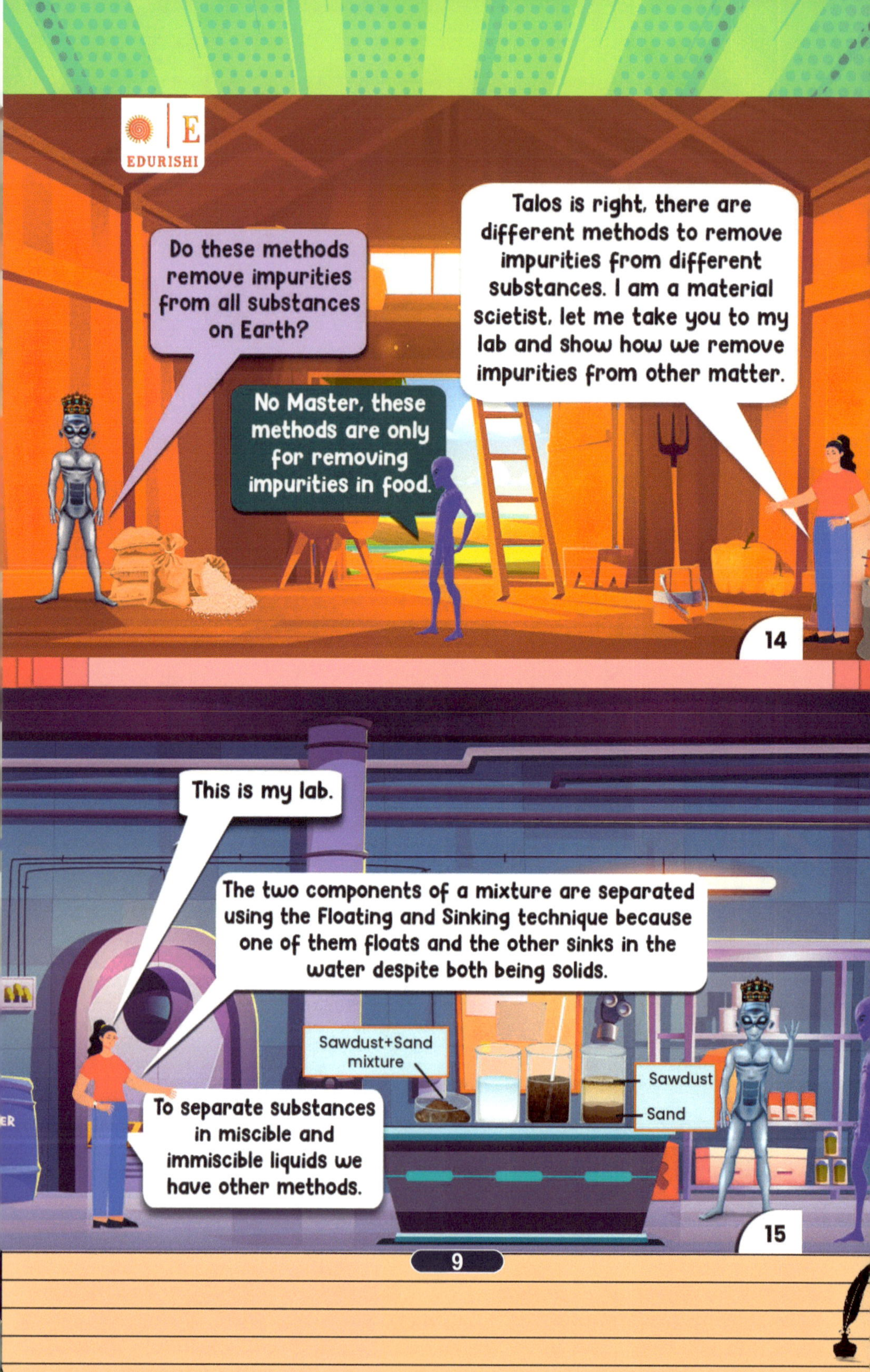

EDURISHI
Do these methods remove impurities from all substances on Earth?
Talos is right, there are different methods to remove impurities from different substances. I am a material scietist, let me take you to my lab and show how we remove impurities from other matter.
No Master, these methods are only for removing impurities in food.
14
This is my lab.
The two components of a mixture are separated using the Floating and Sinking technique because one of them floats and the other sinks in the water despite both being solids.
Sawdust+Sand mixture
Sawdust
Sand
To separate substances in miscible and immiscible liquids we have other methods.
15
9

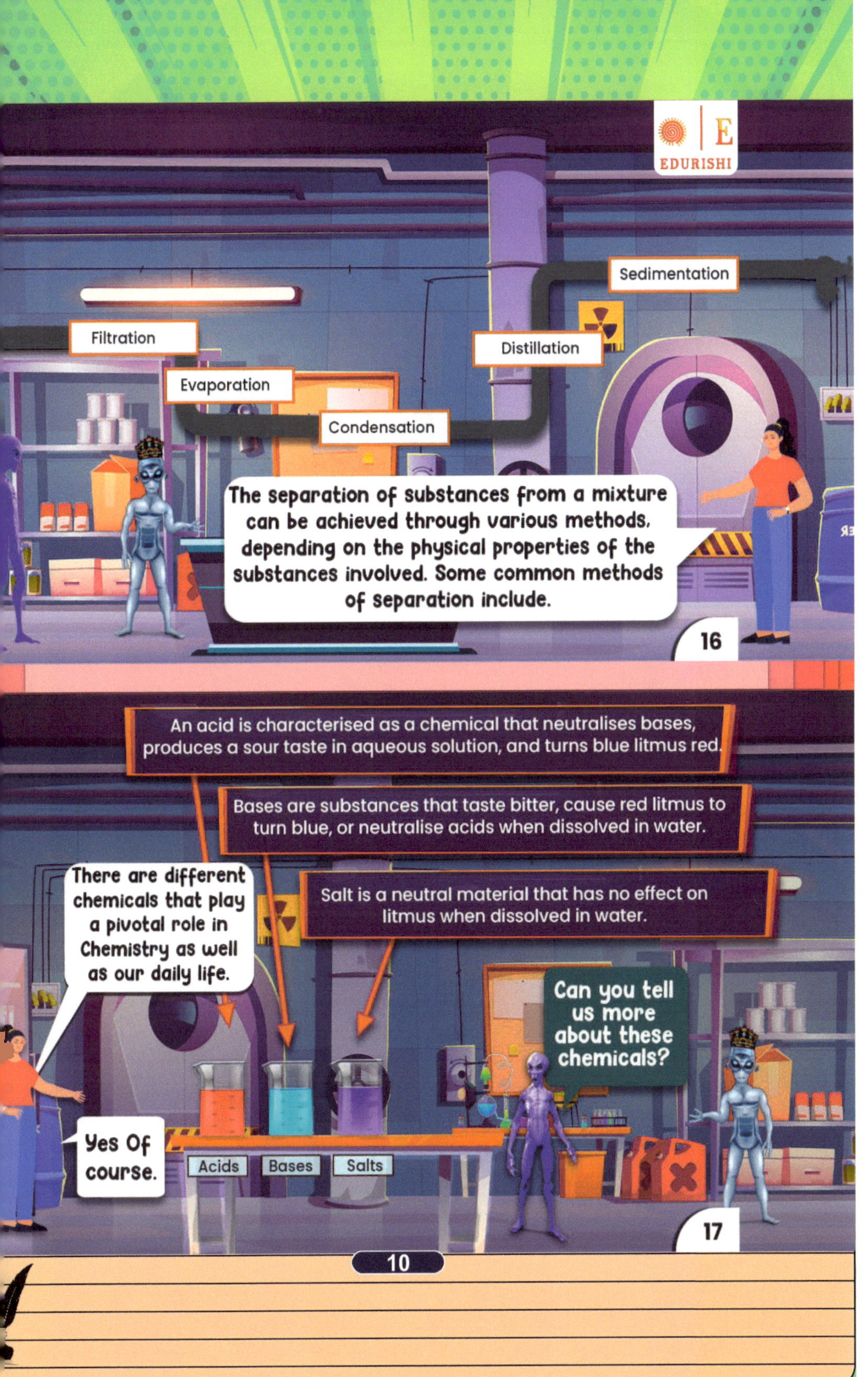
EDURISHI
Sedimentation
Filtration
Distillation
Evaporation
Condensation
The separation of substances from a mixture can be achieved through various methods, depending on the physical properties of the substances involved. Some common methods of separation include.
16
An acid is characterised as a chemical that neutralises bases, produces a sour taste in aqueous solution, and turns blue litmus red.
Bases are substances that taste bitter, cause red litmus to turn blue, or neutralise acids when dissolved in water.
There are different chemicals that play a pivotal role in Chemistry as well as our daily life.
Salt is a neutral material that has no effect on litmus when dissolved in water.
Can you tell us more about these chemicals?
Yes Of course.
Acids
Bases
Salts
17
10

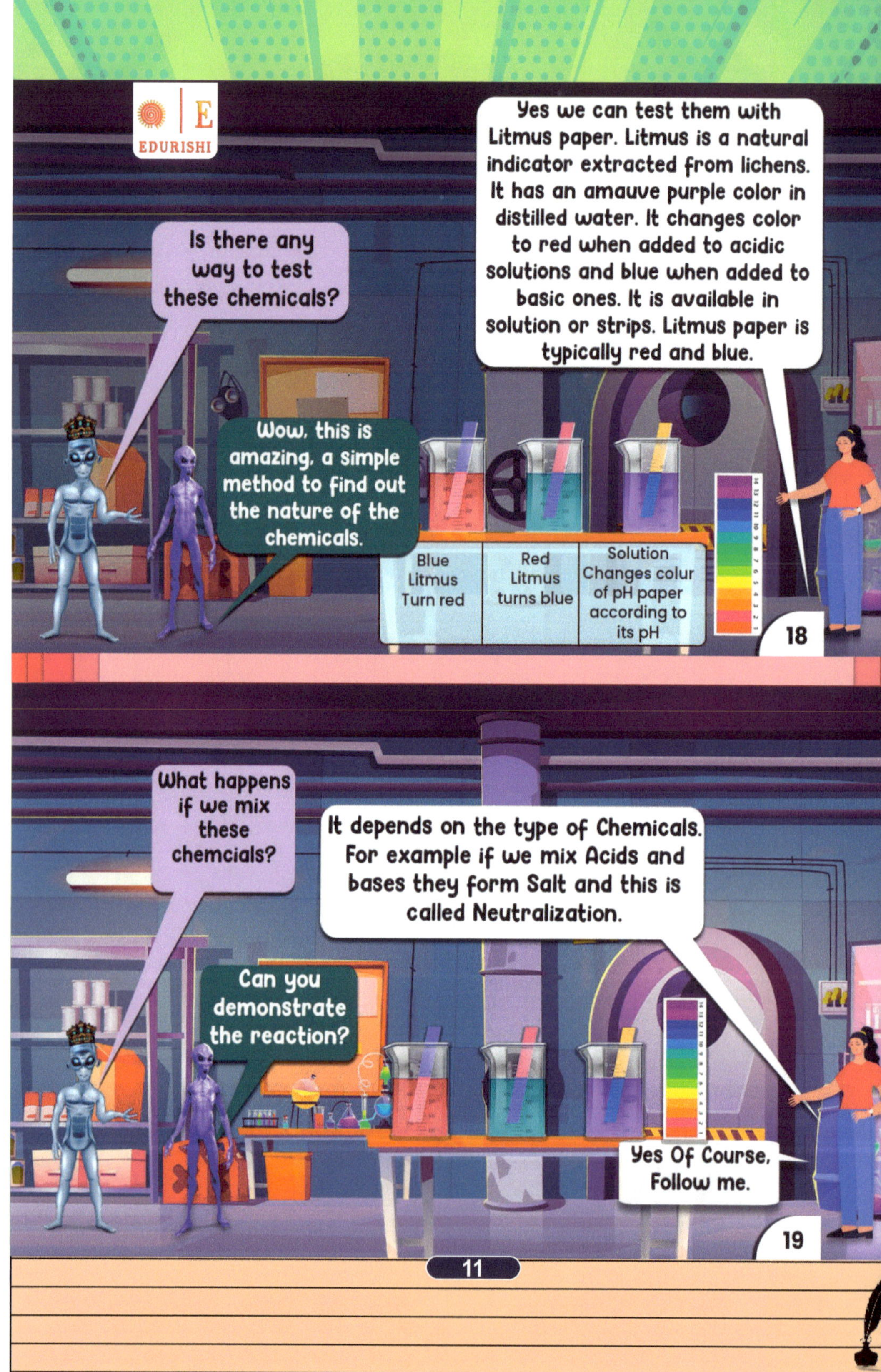

EDURISHI
Is there any way to test these chemicals?
Yes we can test them with Litmus paper. Litmus is a natural indicator extracted from lichens. It has an amauve purple color in distilled water. It changes color to red when added to acidic solutions and blue when added to basic ones. It is available in solution or strips. Litmus paper is typically red and blue.
Wow, this is amazing, a simple method to find out the nature of the chemicals.
Blue Litmus Turn red
Red Litmus turns blue
Solution Changes colur of pH paper according to its pH
18
What happens if we mix these chemcials?
It depends on the type of Chemicals. For example if we mix Acids and bases they form Salt and this is called Neutralization.
Can you demonstrate the reaction?
Yes Of Course, Follow me.
19
11

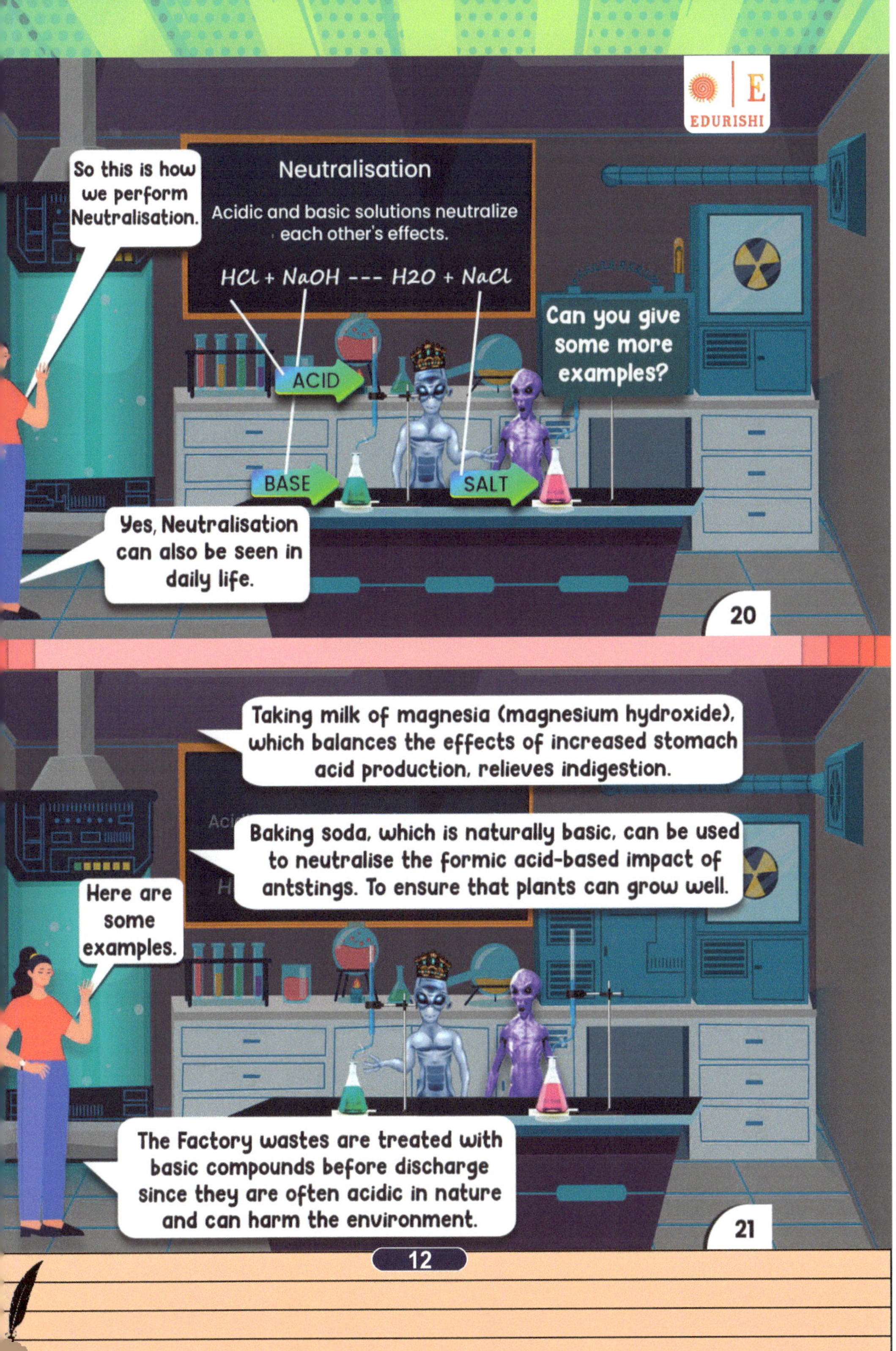

So this is how we perform Neutralisation.

Neutralisation
Acidic and basic solutions neutralize each other's effects.

HCl + NaOH --- H2O + NaCl

Can you give some more examples?

ACID

BASE

SALT

Yes, Neutralisation can also be seen in daily life.

20

Taking milk of magnesia (magnesium hydroxide), which balances the effects of increased stomach acid production, relieves indigestion.

Baking soda, which is naturally basic, can be used to neutralise the formic acid-based impact of antstings. To ensure that plants can grow well.

Here are some examples.

The Factory wastes are treated with basic compounds before discharge since they are often acidic in nature and can harm the environment.

21

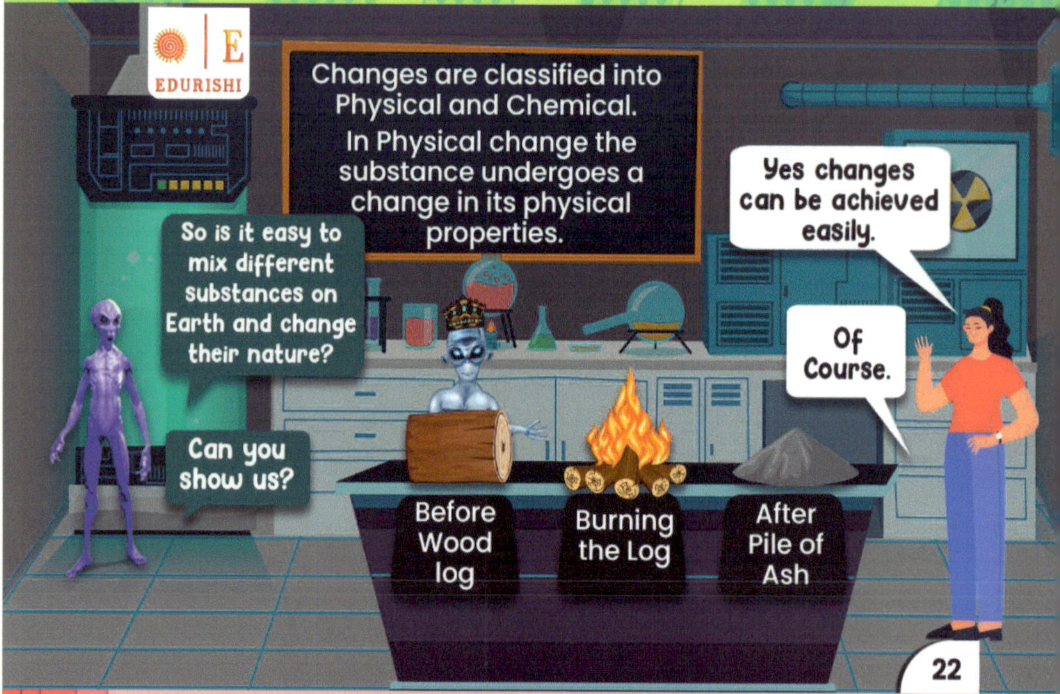

Changes are classified into Physical and Chemical. In Physical change the substance undergoes a change in its physical properties.
So is it easy to mix different substances on Earth and change their nature?
Can you show us?
Yes changes can be achieved easily.
Of Course.
Before Wood log
Burning the Log
After Pile of Ash
22

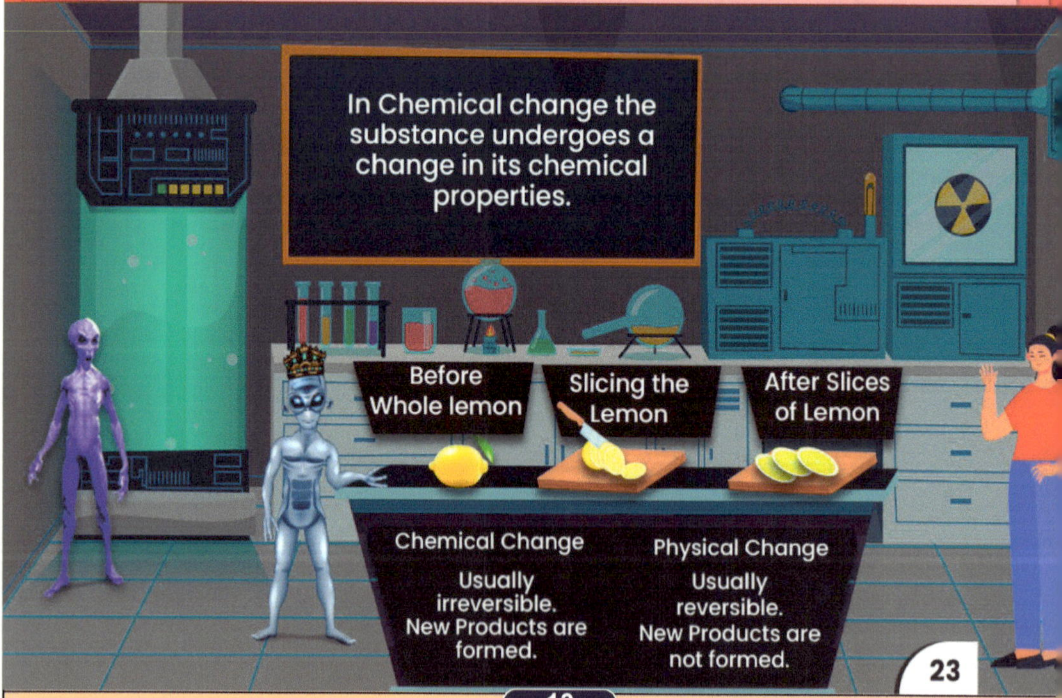

In Chemical change the substance undergoes a change in its chemical properties.
Before Whole lemon
Slicing the Lemon
After Slices of Lemon
Chemical Change
Usually irreversible. New Products are formed.
Physical Change
Usually reversible. New Products are not formed.
23

Changes are of vital importance in our everyday life. These changes are important to sustain life. For Example Plants prepare their own food by a process called photosynthesis, which is a chemical change.
But what do you achieve by these changes?
Yes, master I have seen how humans have created new substances for their survival. We must learn this.
We can also create new substances which make our lives easier. Let me take you to a place nearby to show how we create new materials.
Yes, this craft will be essential for Onidurans.
24
But where are we going?
I am taking you to a factory to show how we use physical and chemical process to make clothes by using different materials in nature.
We are going to a clothes factory.
But why?
As you already know that the three essential necessities of a human being are food, clothing, and shelter. Clothing is the second essential item for humans after food. To shield our bodies from the effects of the weather, we need to wear clothes.
25
14

Mr Zorg, this is my friend Oliver. He works in a clothes factory.
We don't have clothes on Onidura as we don't know the craft of making clothes from different materials, so thanks for your help.
Welcome to Earth Mr Zorg. Talos has told us about your planet and I am here to help you with all the information about clothes.
Even on Earth, there was a time when there were no clothes and people covered their bodies with leaves, hide, fur and feathers from birds but today we have mastered the art of making clothes from different materials.
26
What you are seeing here are the fabric (cloth). All cloth materials are made up of long, narrow, thin structures called fibres. Fibres are obtained from natural as well as man-made sources.
But which fibres do you use?
Natural fibres are obtained from plants and animals while synthetic fibres are made of chemicals.
Here in this factory we use only Natural fibres. Let me show you.
27
15

These are some Natural fibres we use Cotton and Jute are obtained from Plants while Silk and Wool are obtained from animals.
EDURISHI
Every Fibre has their Unique method of processing. We have designated machinery for these tasks.
How do you turn these Fibres into Clothes?
It is not possible to show all of them but I can show you the processing of Cotton and Jute.
Can you show us?
COTTON
WOOL
JUTE
28
Here we process Cotton which involves 6 steps from Plucking to Stitching.
Spinning
Carding
Weaving
Knitting
Plucking & Ginning
Stitching
This is fascinating. With this we can make large quantities of clothes in very less time.
TON
29
16

EDURISHI
This cotton fibre is very useful. Tell me more about it.
Cotton is the most widely used Fibre on Earth.
Cotton has various uses such as:- Fabric, Women and Baby Care, Consumer Products,Cosmetics, Agriculture.
COTTON
JUTE
30
Retting of plants
Stripping of plants
Washing and Drying
Jute is processed in the following manner:
Jute is used in making Strings Cords, Carpets Rugs, Bags.
Jute is another valuable Natural Fibre. Lets learn about that.
31
17

Master, Humans have such factories everywhere where they make different objects from such materials.
This craft will be very useful for us. Go and bring Master Scientist here.
These materials, these machines are very useful.
32
Scan for Material Video
Master Koda there is so much to learn on Earth. I want you to work with humans and learn their craft.
Welcome Mr Koda, I am Sophie.
If you want to learn about making new objects then you will have to come to my lab to first learn about materials.
At your service master Zorg.
33
18

EDURISHI
To make any object we need raw materials. Nature has given us many materials which we call Matter.
Why such difference in their Structure?
Attraction between, molecules is not so strong hence they are loosely packed and don't have a definite shape but have a definite volume.
This is due to different arrangement of Molecules.
SOLID
LIQUID
GAS
Attraction between molecules is very strong hence they are tightly packed and have definite shape and volume.
Attraction between molecules is negligible hence they are far apart and move freely and don't have a definite volume and shape.
34
There are different materials here like Metal rods, glass beakers, plastic chair and water.
But how do you distinguish these materials?
Water
Metal
Glass
Wood
Plastic
Every matter has their own unique properties which makes them different.
35

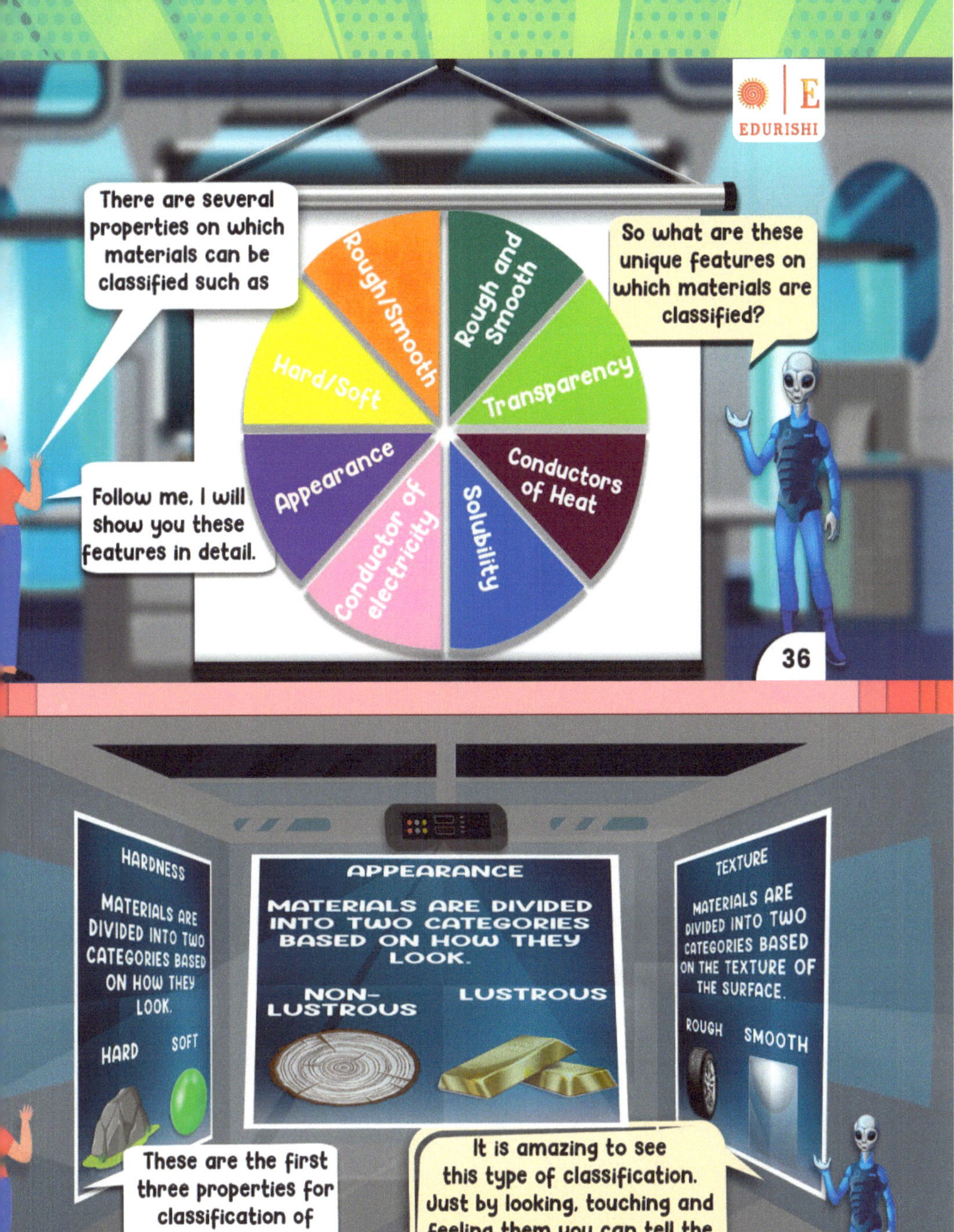
There are several properties on which materials can be classified such as
Follow me, I will show you these features in detail.
So what are these unique features on which materials are classified?
Rough/Smooth
Rough and Smooth
Hard/Soft
Transparency
Appearance
Conductors of Heat
Conductor of electricity
Solubility
36
HARDNESS
MATERIALS ARE DIVIDED INTO TWO CATEGORIES BASED ON HOW THEY LOOK.
HARD
SOFT
APPEARANCE
MATERIALS ARE DIVIDED INTO TWO CATEGORIES BASED ON HOW THEY LOOK.
NON-LUSTROUS
LUSTROUS
TEXTURE
MATERIALS ARE DIVIDED INTO TWO CATEGORIES BASED ON THE TEXTURE OF THE SURFACE.
ROUGH
SMOOTH
These are the first three properties for classification of materials.
It is amazing to see this type of classification. Just by looking, touching and feeling them you can tell the type of material.
37

EDURISHI

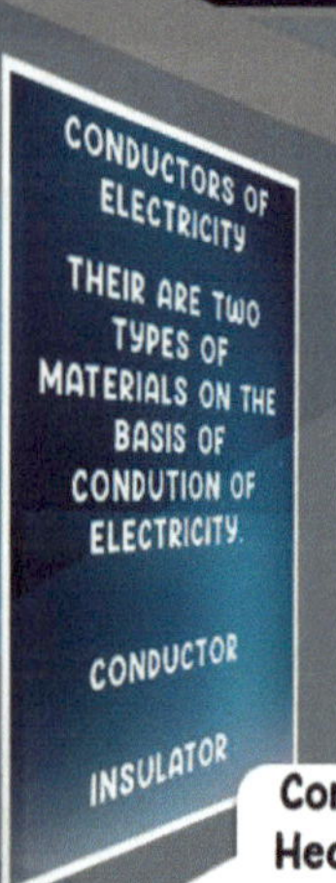

TRANSPARENCY
BASED ON TRANSPARENCY THE MATERIALS ARE CLASSIFIED INTO 3 TYPES.
TRANSPATRENT
OPAQUE
TRANSLUCENT
SOLUBILITY
BASED ON TRANSPARENCY THE MATERIALS ARE OF 2 TYPES.
SOLUBLE
INSOLUBLE
SUGAR
FLOTATION
BASED ON THEIR FLOATING ABILITY THE MATERIALS ARE OF 2 TYPES.
MATERIALS WHICH FLOAT ON WATER
MATERIALS WHICH SINK IN WATER
The next three properties are Transparency, Solubility and Flotation.
Wow, Sophie amazing to see how some materials float while some dissolve into water.
38

CONDUCTORS OF ELECTRICITY
THEIR ARE TWO TYPES OF MATERIALS ON THE BASIS OF CONDUTION OF ELECTRICITY.
CONDUCTOR
INSULATOR
CONDUCTOR
Gold –
INSULATOR
Wood –
GOOD CONDUCTOR
Silver –
BAD CONDUCTOR
Cork –
CONDUCTORS OF HEAT
TWO TYPES OF MATERIALS ON THE BASIS OF THEIR ABILITY TO CONDUCT HEAT.
GOOD CONDUCTOR
BAD CONDUCTOR
Conduction of Electricity and Heat are another property to classify materials.
That's spot on!
I think it means that electricity can flow through it easily, like in metals.
39

GROUPING OF MATERIALS
ON THE BASIS OF THEIR COMMON PROPERTIES.
LIVING THINGS
NON-LIVING THINGS
GROUPING OF MATERIALS ON THE BASIS OF THEIR ORIGIN OF MATERIAL.
OBJECTS COMING FROM PLANTS
SEED
OBJECTS COMING FROM ANIMALS
MEAT
OBJECTS COMING FROM EARTH
MARBLE
GROUPING OF MATERIALS ON THE BASIS OF THEIR GROSS PROPERTIES AND USE OF MATERIALS.
HARDNESS
TRANSPARENCY
Not only this we can also group these materials based on their characteristics for similar use.
I am very excited to learn about this.
40
Does that mean all these properties and features of materials are fixed and can never change.
Materials have their unique properties but one material can be changed into other because change is the rule of nature.
Is this how you use these materials and make new materials from them?
Yes.
41

EDURISHI

CHANGE IN COLOUR
SKY IS BLUE DURING DAY
SKY IS DARK DURING NIGHT
CHANGE IN SHAPE
VISIBLE SHAPE OF THE MOON CHANGES FROM DAY TOP DAY.
CHANGE IN POSITION
SUN RISING IN THE EAST AND SETTING IN THE WEST.
Not only this we can also group these materials based on their characteristics for similar use.
We're putting them into groups based on how we can use them!
42
CHANGE IN SEASON
SUMMER
AUTUMN
WINTER
SPRING
CHANGE IN TEMPERATURE
FEELING HOT
FEELING COLD
CHANGE IN SIZE
A SEED GERMINATE INTO SAPLING, SAPLING GROW INTO A SMALL PLANT.
When we group materials based on their common properties, it helps us understand them better and use them wisely.
yes.
43
23

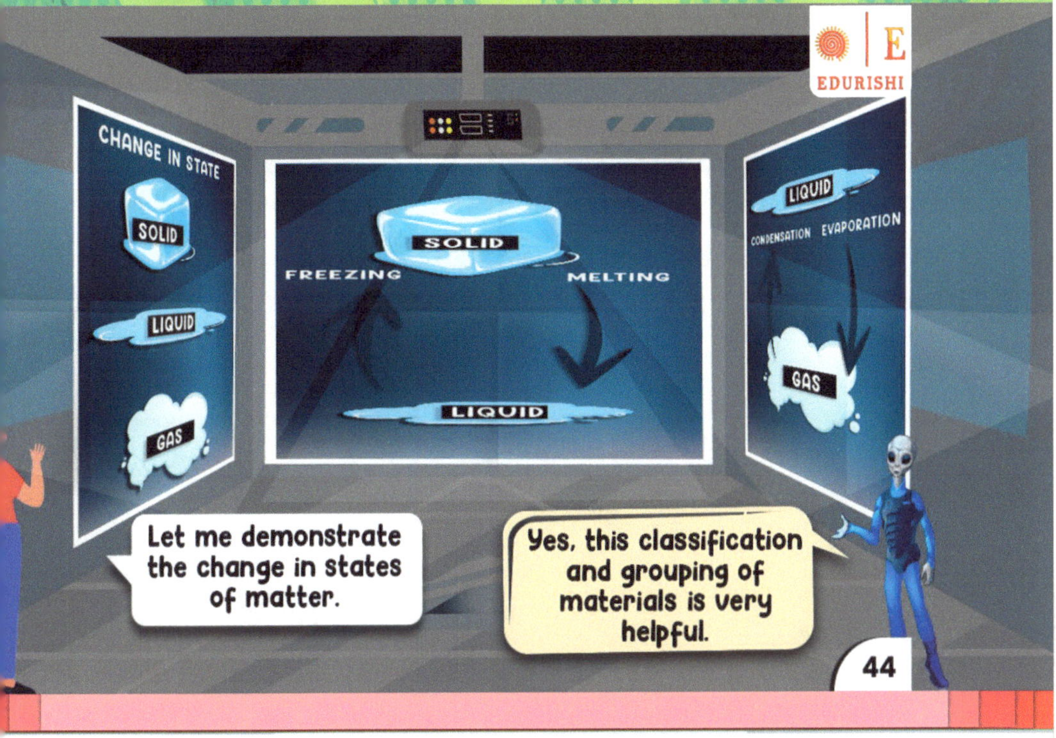

CHANGE IN STATE
SOLID
LIQUID
GAS
FREEZING
SOLID
MELTING
LIQUID
LIQUID
CONDENSATION
EVAPORATION
GAS
EDURISHI
Let me demonstrate the change in states of matter.
Yes, this classification and grouping of materials is very helpful.
44

This is how the state of a matter can be changed.
These changes makes our life easier, like boiling or cooling water according to our need, cooking food. There are plenty of examples where changes help us in our daily life.
How are these changes helpful in your day to day life?
To answer this first I have to demonstrate these changes, so follow me to my lab.
So are these changes permanent?
45

EDURISHI
Changes can be classified in two :
Reversible – Changed form can be obtained back by reversing cause of change
Irreversible – New substance is formed and cause of change cant be reversed to get the original substance.
What kind of change was the changing of states of water?
Ice can be converted into water by melting, water can be converted into steam by boiling and the steam can be condensed to get back the liquid also the liquid can be freezed to get back ice, so this is a reversible change.
46
There are two situations, 1st is burning of a candle and 2nd is melting of wax. Now tell me which of these two is reversible and irreversible?
Yes, burning is involved in both but the burning of a candle is an irreversible change.
I can't figure it out because in both something is burning.
As it can't regain its previous state while melting of wax only converts solid wax into liquid. Which can again converted into solid so it is a reversible change.
47
25

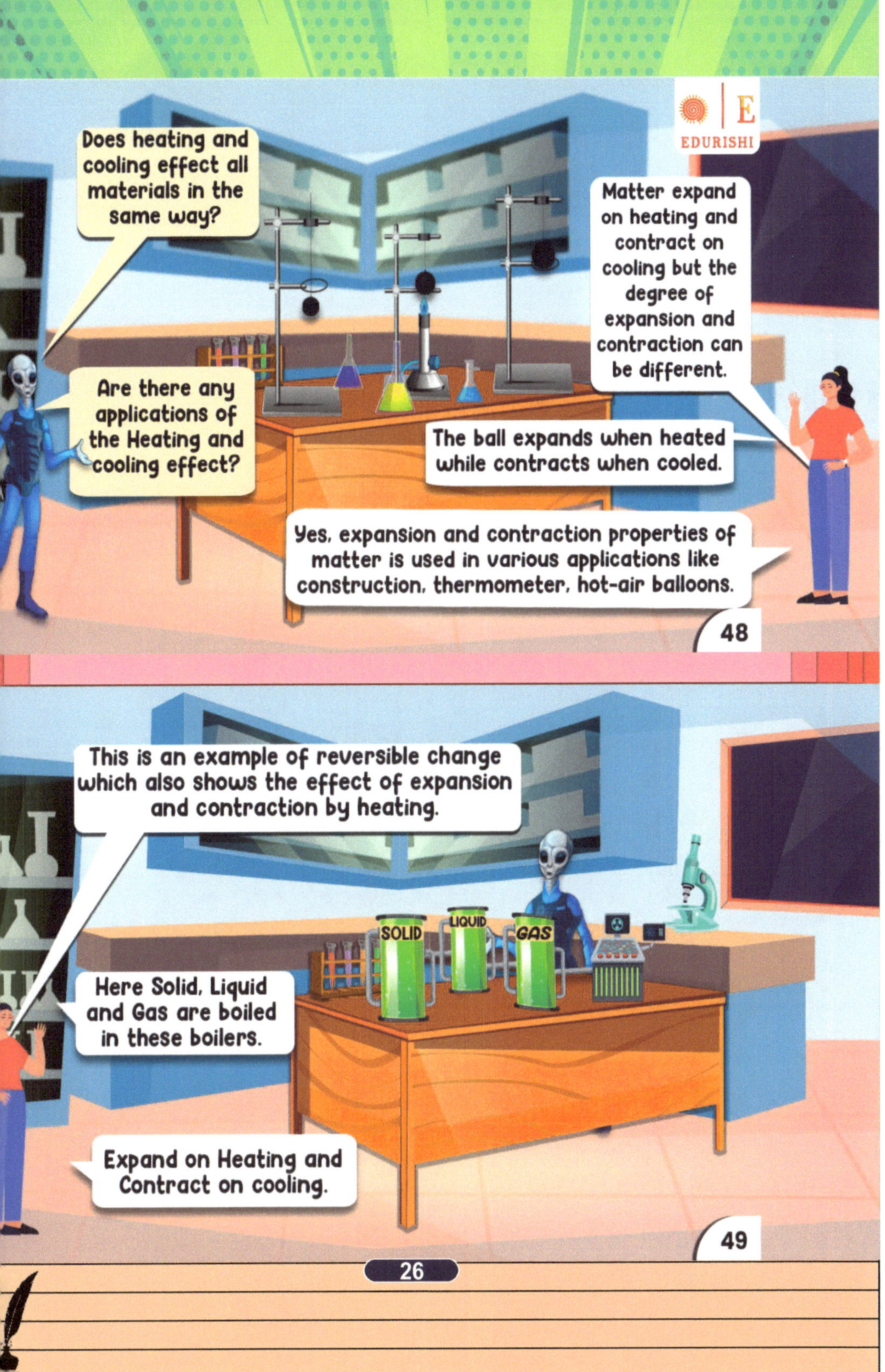
Does heating and cooling effect all materials in the same way?
Matter expand on heating and contract on cooling but the degree of expansion and contraction can be different.
Are there any applications of the Heating and cooling effect?
The ball expands when heated while contracts when cooled.
Yes, expansion and contraction properties of matter is used in various applications like construction, thermometer, hot-air balloons.
48
This is an example of reversible change which also shows the effect of expansion and contraction by heating.
SOLID
LIQUID
GAS
Here Solid, Liquid and Gas are boiled in these boilers.
Expand on Heating and Contract on cooling.
49
EDURISHI

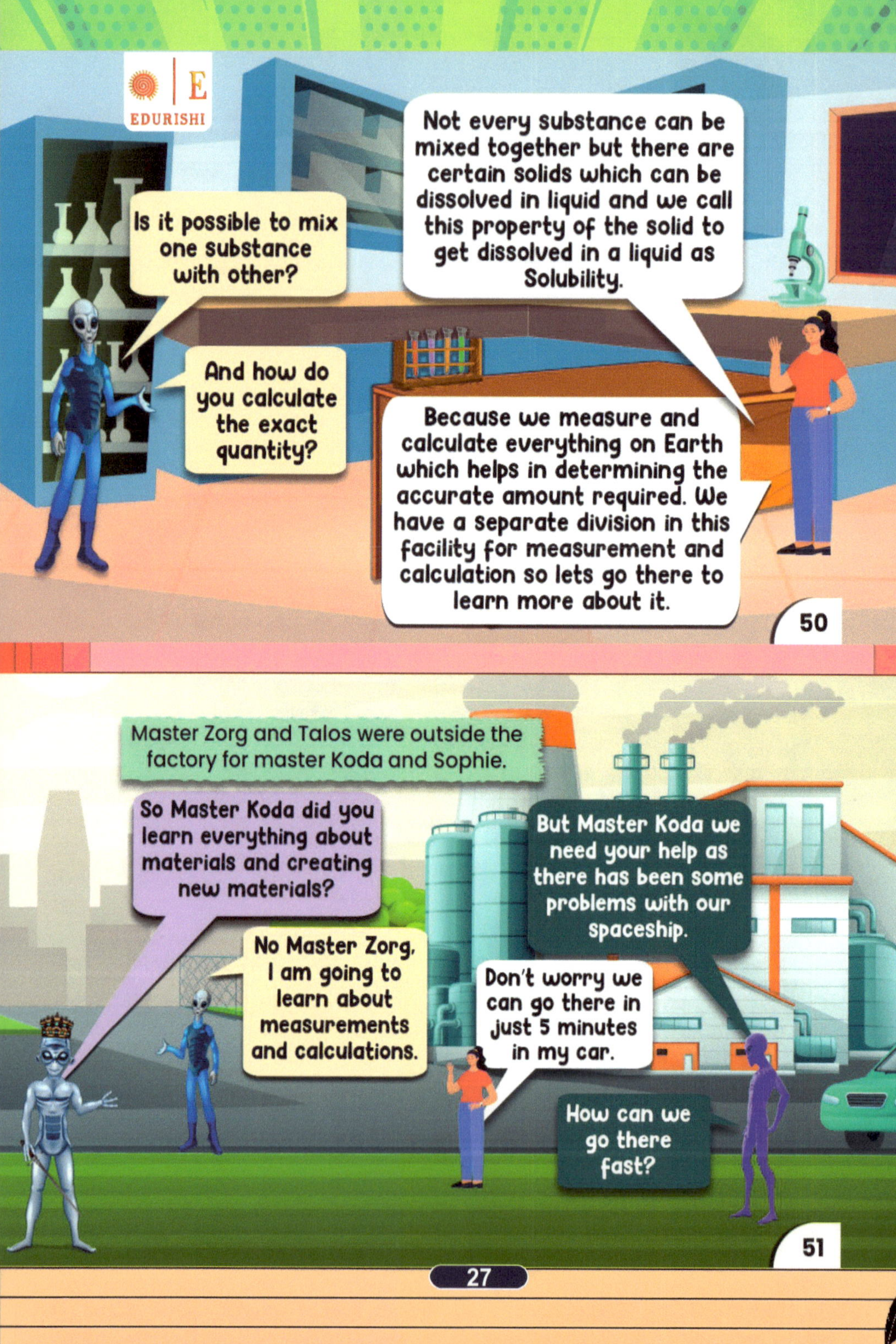
EDURISHI
Is it possible to mix one substance with other?
Not every substance can be mixed together but there are certain solids which can be dissolved in liquid and we call this property of the solid to get dissolved in a liquid as Solubility.
And how do you calculate the exact quantity?
Because we measure and calculate everything on Earth which helps in determining the accurate amount required. We have a separate division in this facility for measurement and calculation so lets go there to learn more about it.
50
Master Zorg and Talos were outside the factory for master Koda and Sophie.
So Master Koda did you learn everything about materials and creating new materials?
But Master Koda we need your help as there has been some problems with our spaceship.
No Master Zorg, I am going to learn about measurements and calculations.
Don't worry we can go there in just 5 minutes in my car.
How can we go there fast?
51
27

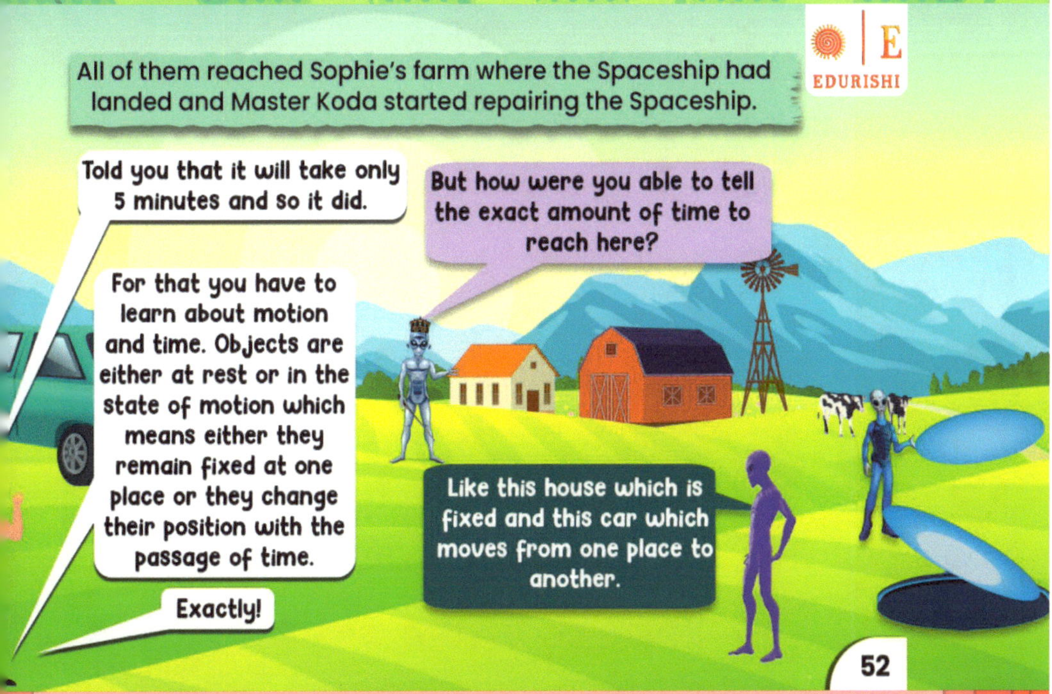

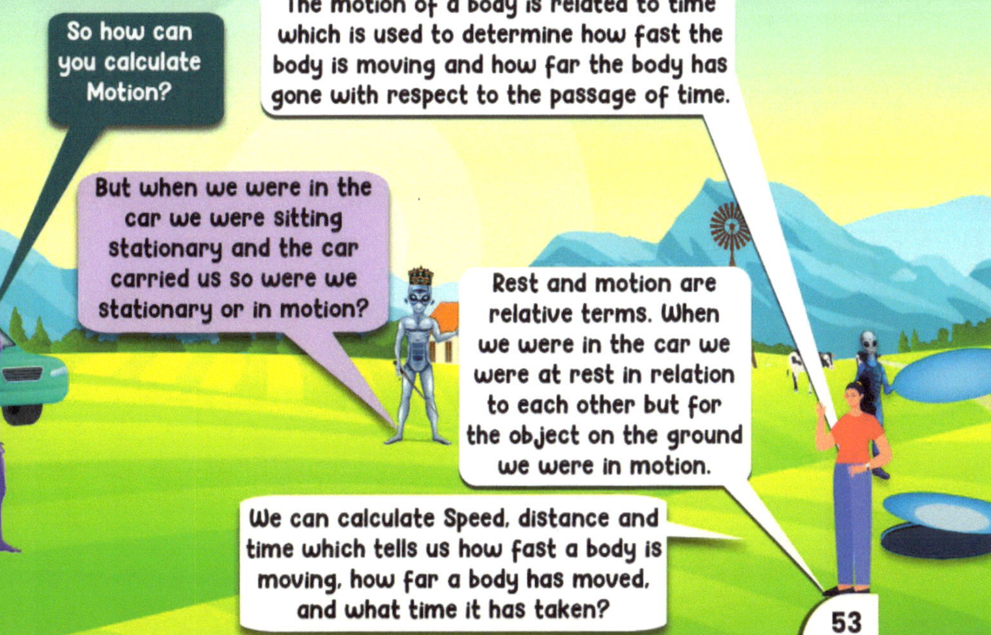

All of them reached Sophie's farm where the Spaceship had landed and Master Koda started repairing the Spaceship.
Told you that it will take only 5 minutes and so it did.
But how were you able to tell the exact amount of time to reach here?
For that you have to learn about motion and time. Objects are either at rest or in the state of motion which means either they remain fixed at one place or they change their position with the passage of time.
Like this house which is fixed and this car which moves from one place to another.
Exactly!

So how can you calculate Motion?
The motion of a body is related to time which is used to determine how fast the body is moving and how far the body has gone with respect to the passage of time.
But when we were in the car we were sitting stationary and the car carried us so were we stationary or in motion?
Rest and motion are relative terms. When we were in the car we were at rest in relation to each other but for the object on the ground we were in motion.
We can calculate Speed, distance and time which tells us how fast a body is moving, how far a body has moved, and what time it has taken?

EDURISHI

How do you calculate the distance?
What tools do you use to measure the distance?
Distance is the space between two points. To understand distance first learn about length which is a measure of how long a thing is from end to end. Suppose if you want to measure the length of this car then you have to find the distance between Point A and B.
We have various tools like scales length tape, scales but first you must know about the unit.
54
In early days, people used to measure lenght with the help of various parts of body.
Four Fingers
One cubit
One handspan
One pace
Observation and estimate were used to measure things in ancient times. Non-standard units of measurement like foot span, footsteps were later used.
A
B
55

EDURISHI

Standard unit of measurement were later adopted to overcome the errors of non-standard unit of measurement.
Metre is the standard unit to measure both "Length" and "Distance". Short form of 'metre' is 'm. Sub units of length are Millimetre = 1/1000th of metre. Centimetre = 1/100th of metre. Higher unit is Kilometre 1 Km = 1000 metre
56

Placing scale along the length to be measured.
To measure length we use tools like scales or length tape. There are certain rules for writing units.
A unit is represented alone. For instance, 1 metre or 10 metre. A unit's abbreviation is frequently written in tiny letters/s-mm, cm, m, km. A unit's short form is also in a singular form. Not in the plural. Unless at the conclusion of a phrase, the short form of a unit should not be followed by a full-stop (.).
57

How do you measure the length of a curved line?
It is not possible to measure the distance of a curved surface using a scale so use a piece of thread.
Measuring the length of a curved line with the help of thread.
A
F
B
E
C
D
58
Like the length motion is not always linear or in a straight line. There are different kinds of motion like:
Master its getting late and dark. Let's go and check the status of the repair work in the spaceship.
Thank you, this is a very useful information for our Onidura.
MOTIONS
1 Linear motion
2 Periodic motion
3 Curvilinear motion
4 Oscillatory motion
5 Non periodic motion
6 Resultant motion
7 Circular motion
8 Random motion
9 Mixed motion
59
31
EDURISHI

Sophie, Zorg and Talos came inside the spaceship where Master Koda was repairing it.
Oh, it is so dark in here. Don't you have powerful light?
On Onidura we get light only from our Sun and from some illuminating rocks which we have fixed in our spaceship for light but they are not powerful.
I will tell you about Light but first please come to my house I have many portable light sources which can bring here to do the repair.
Compared to this spaceship there was so much Light in your factory and lab so how do you get that amount of Light?
60

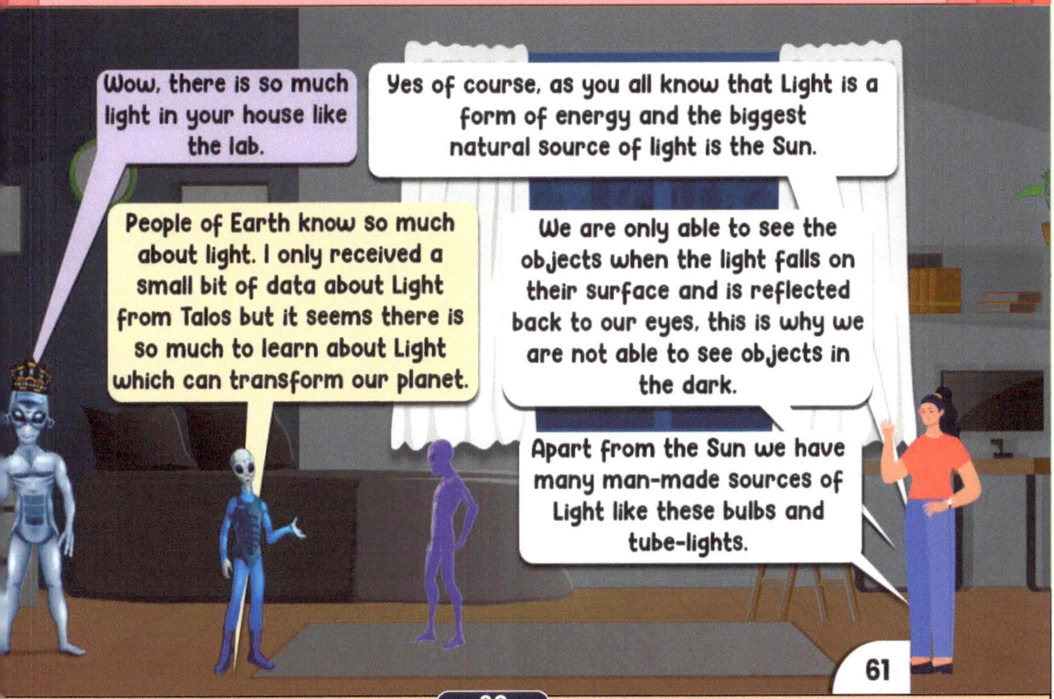

Wow, there is so much light in your house like the lab.
Yes of course, as you all know that Light is a form of energy and the biggest natural source of light is the Sun.
People of Earth know so much about light. I only received a small bit of data about Light from Talos but it seems there is so much to learn about Light which can transform our planet.
We are only able to see the objects when the light falls on their surface and is reflected back to our eyes, this is why we are not able to see objects in the dark.
Apart from the Sun we have many man-made sources of Light like these bulbs and tube-lights.
61

EDURISHI
Scan for Reflection of Light Video
Don't you have luminous objects on Earth?
Sun, Star, flame are the only natural luminous object, this is why we have created many artificial luminous objects to provide us Light.
Moon is shining in the sky so can we consider moon as a luminous object?
No moon is not a luminous object because it shines with the light from the sun.
Come with me, I want to show you something.
62
TRANSPARENT
TRANSLUCENT
OPAQUE
If light passes through them
If part of Light passes through them
If no Light passes through them
These are the three windows.
1st is transparent as you can see outside.
2nd is translucent as the outside is not completely visible.
3rd is opaque because the window is closed so you can't see outside.
Yes I have learnt about them from Talos that the objects are classified on the basis of how light interact with them.
33
63

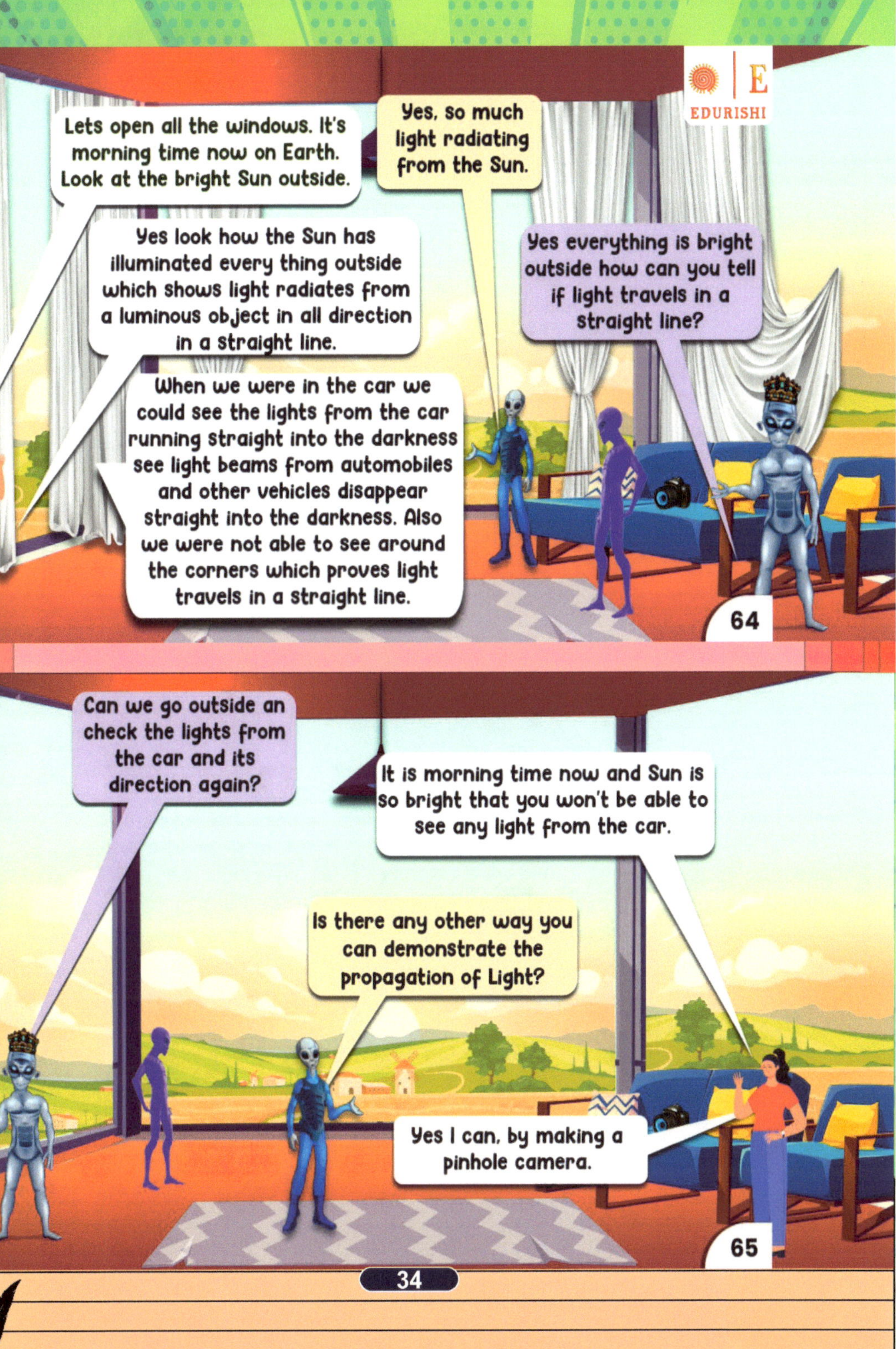

Lets open all the windows. It's morning time now on Earth. Look at the bright Sun outside.
Yes, so much light radiating from the Sun.
Yes look how the Sun has illuminated every thing outside which shows light radiates from a luminous object in all direction in a straight line.
Yes everything is bright outside how can you tell if light travels in a straight line?
When we were in the car we could see the lights from the car running straight into the darkness see light beams from automobiles and other vehicles disappear straight into the darkness. Also we were not able to see around the corners which proves light travels in a straight line.
EDURISHI
64
Can we go outside an check the lights from the car and its direction again?
It is morning time now and Sun is so bright that you won't be able to see any light from the car.
Is there any other way you can demonstrate the propagation of Light?
Yes I can, by making a pinhole camera.
65
34

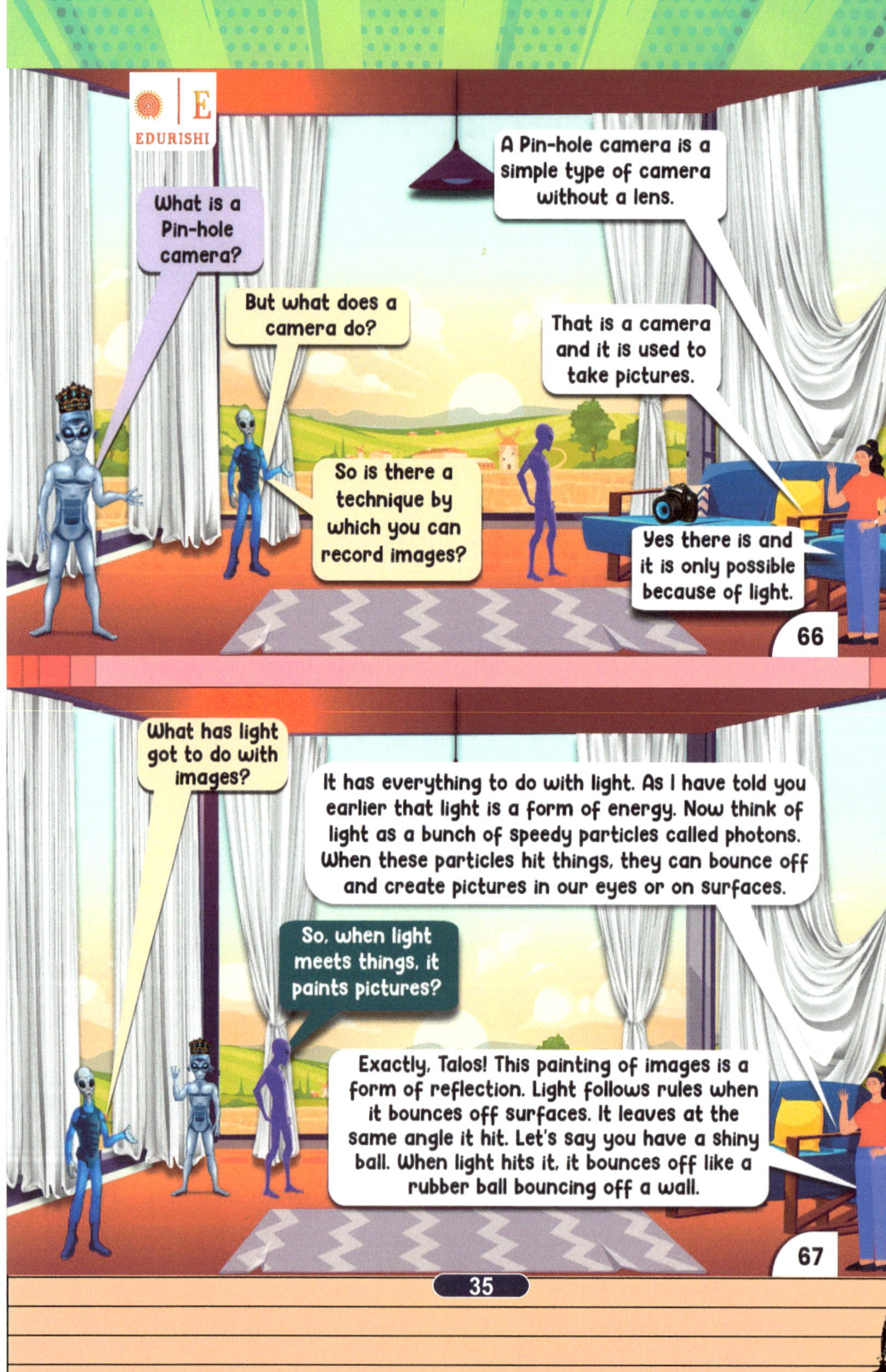

EDURISHI
What is a Pin-hole camera?
A Pin-hole camera is a simple type of camera without a lens.
But what does a camera do?
That is a camera and it is used to take pictures.
So is there a technique by which you can record images?
Yes there is and it is only possible because of light.
66
What has light got to do with images?
It has everything to do with light. As I have told you earlier that light is a form of energy. Now think of light as a bunch of speedy particles called photons. When these particles hit things, they can bounce off and create pictures in our eyes or on surfaces.
So, when light meets things, it paints pictures?
Exactly, Talos! This painting of images is a form of reflection. Light follows rules when it bounces off surfaces. It leaves at the same angle it hit. Let's say you have a shiny ball. When light hits it, it bounces off like a rubber ball bouncing off a wall.
67

Talos, please stand in front of this mirror. What you observe is your reflection which is formed when the light is reflected back to you by this plane glass mirror ..
But there is one difference in the image, the right appears left and left appears right.
Wow, this is me.
Is this the only kind of mirror you have on Earth?
No, We also have curved mirrors which are either convex or concave. Follow me I will show them to you.
68
This is a Concave mirror. That is a Convex mirror.
What is that?
That is a magnifying glass which is used to produce magnified image of an object and it is made of two convex mirrors.
Is that what you call a Lens?
This is what we call a lens. Lens like this magnifying glass, can make things appear larger or smaller by bending light.
69
36

EDURISHI
What is the difference between a lens and a mirror?
Mirror has only one surface which reflect light. Lens has two surfaces out of which one or both can refract light.
So lenses do the opposite of mirrors?
It's truly fascinating how light can be shaped and molded in so many ways.
You got it, Talos! Lenses and mirrors are like partners in shaping how light moves and interacts with the world. They're used in glasses, cameras, telescopes, and even our eyes to help us see better and capture light's beauty.
70
Now in this dark room you will be able to understand the properties of Light properly .
What is that image on the ground?
It looks like the window.
This is the shadow of the window.
So shadow is a region of absence of Light.
How is this formed?
When light meets something it can't pass through, a shadow is formed.
71
37

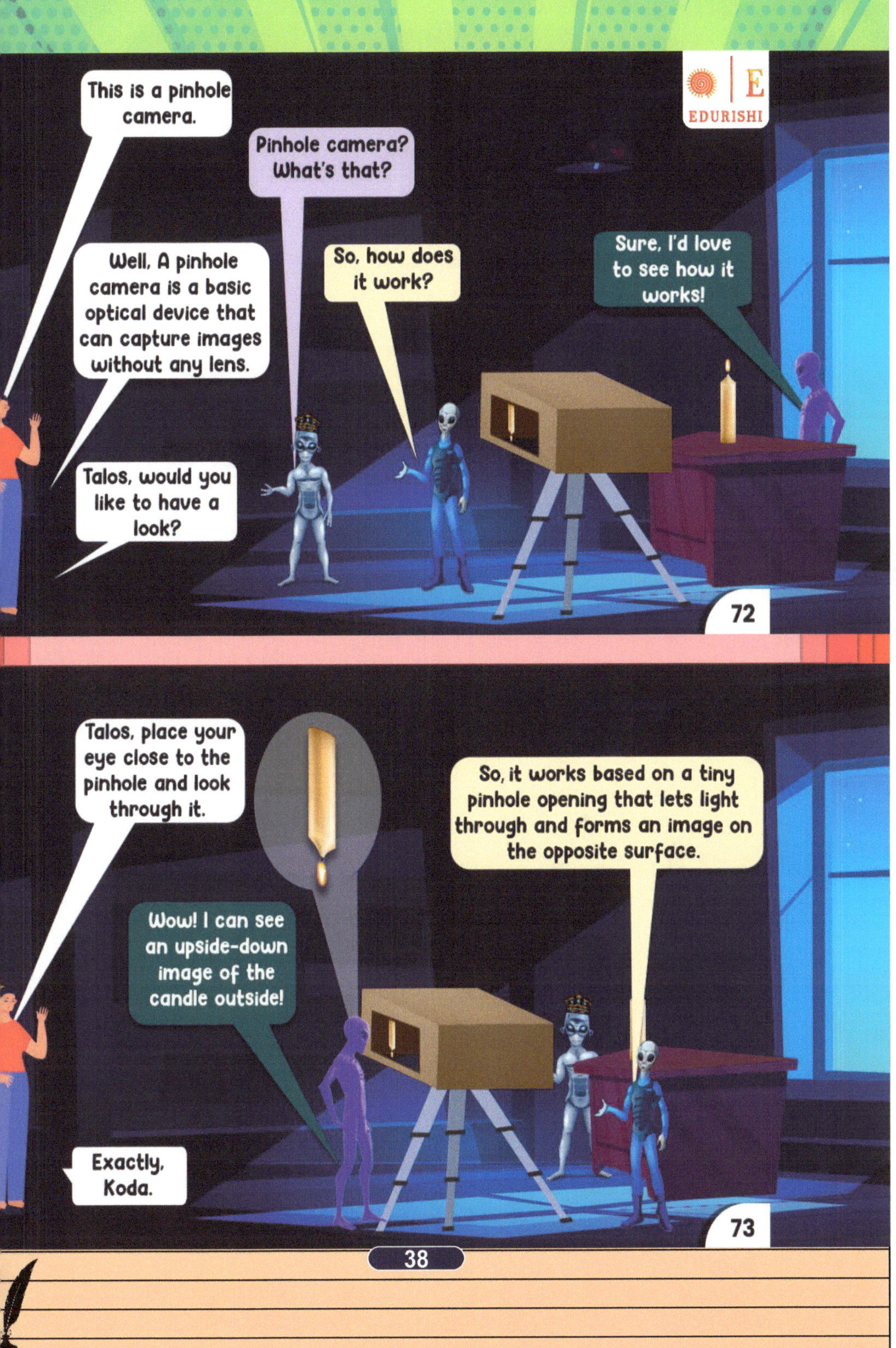

This is a pinhole camera.
Pinhole camera? What's that?
Well, A pinhole camera is a basic optical device that can capture images without any lens.
So, how does it work?
Sure, I'd love to see how it works!
Talos, would you like to have a look?
72
Talos, place your eye close to the pinhole and look through it.
So, it works based on a tiny pinhole opening that lets light through and forms an image on the opposite surface.
Wow! I can see an upside-down image of the candle outside!
Exactly, Koda.
73
EDURISHI

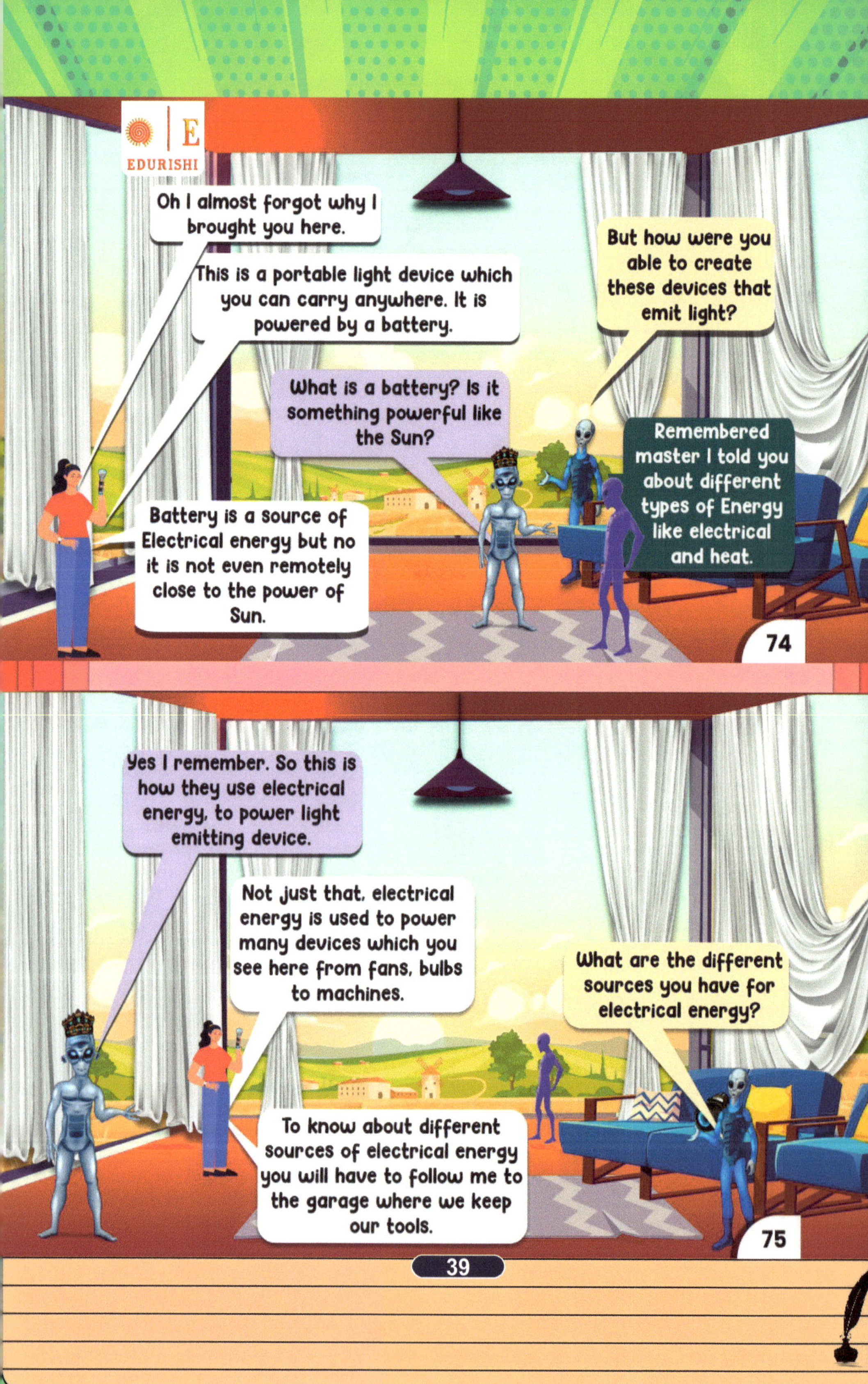
Oh I almost forgot why I brought you here.
This is a portable light device which you can carry anywhere. It is powered by a battery.
But how were you able to create these devices that emit light?
What is a battery? Is it something powerful like the Sun?
Remembered master I told you about different types of Energy like electrical and heat.
Battery is a source of Electrical energy but no it is not even remotely close to the power of Sun.
74
Yes I remember. So this is how they use electrical energy, to power light emitting device.
Not just that, electrical energy is used to power many devices which you see here from fans, bulbs to machines.
What are the different sources you have for electrical energy?
To know about different sources of electrical energy you will have to follow me to the garage where we keep our tools.
75

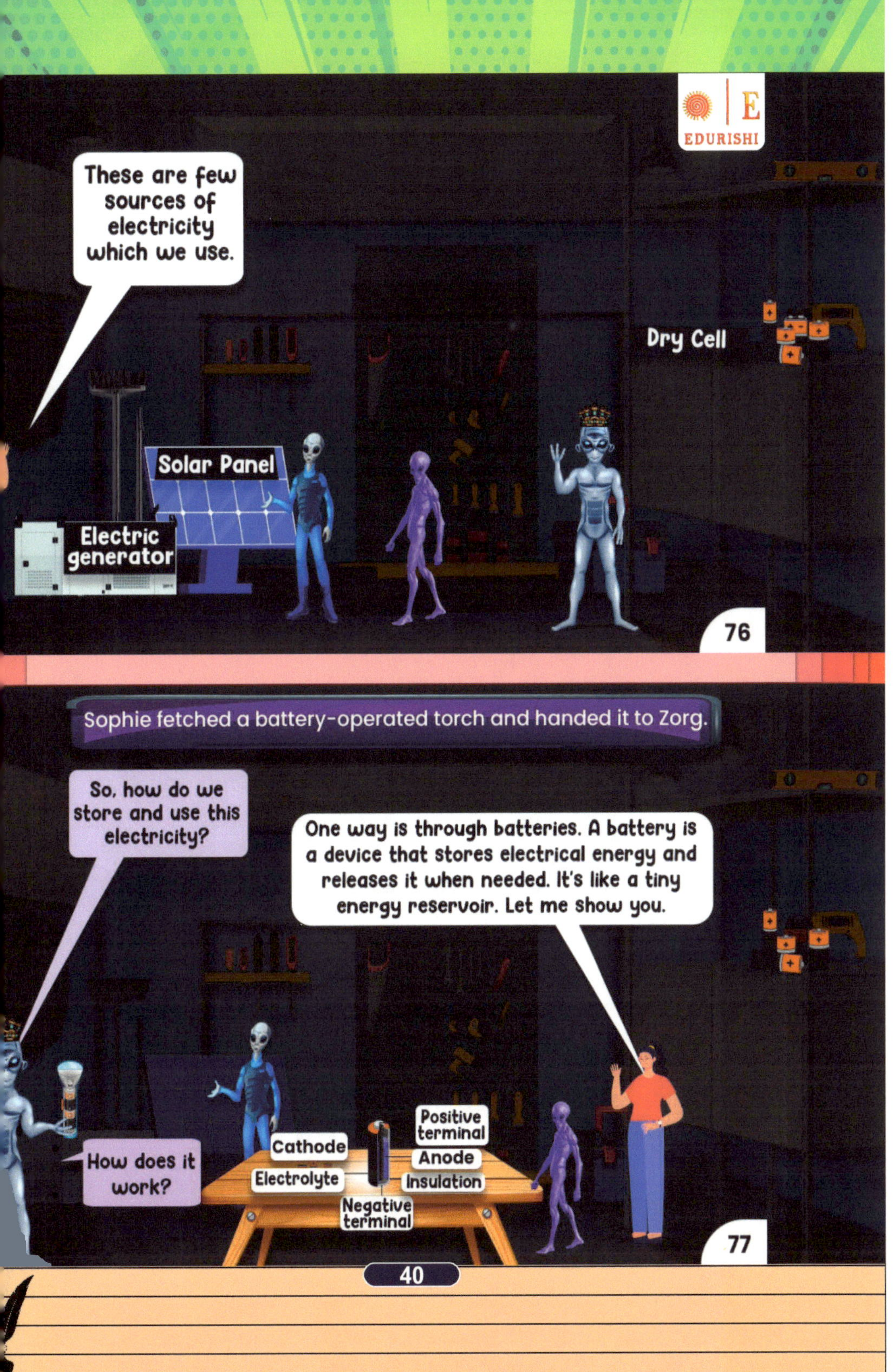
These are few sources of electricity which we use.
Dry Cell
Solar Panel
Electric generator
76
Sophie fetched a battery-operated torch and handed it to Zorg.
So, how do we store and use this electricity?
One way is through batteries. A battery is a device that stores electrical energy and releases it when needed. It's like a tiny energy reservoir. Let me show you.
How does it work?
Cathode
Electrolyte
Positive terminal
Anode
Insulation
Negative terminal
77

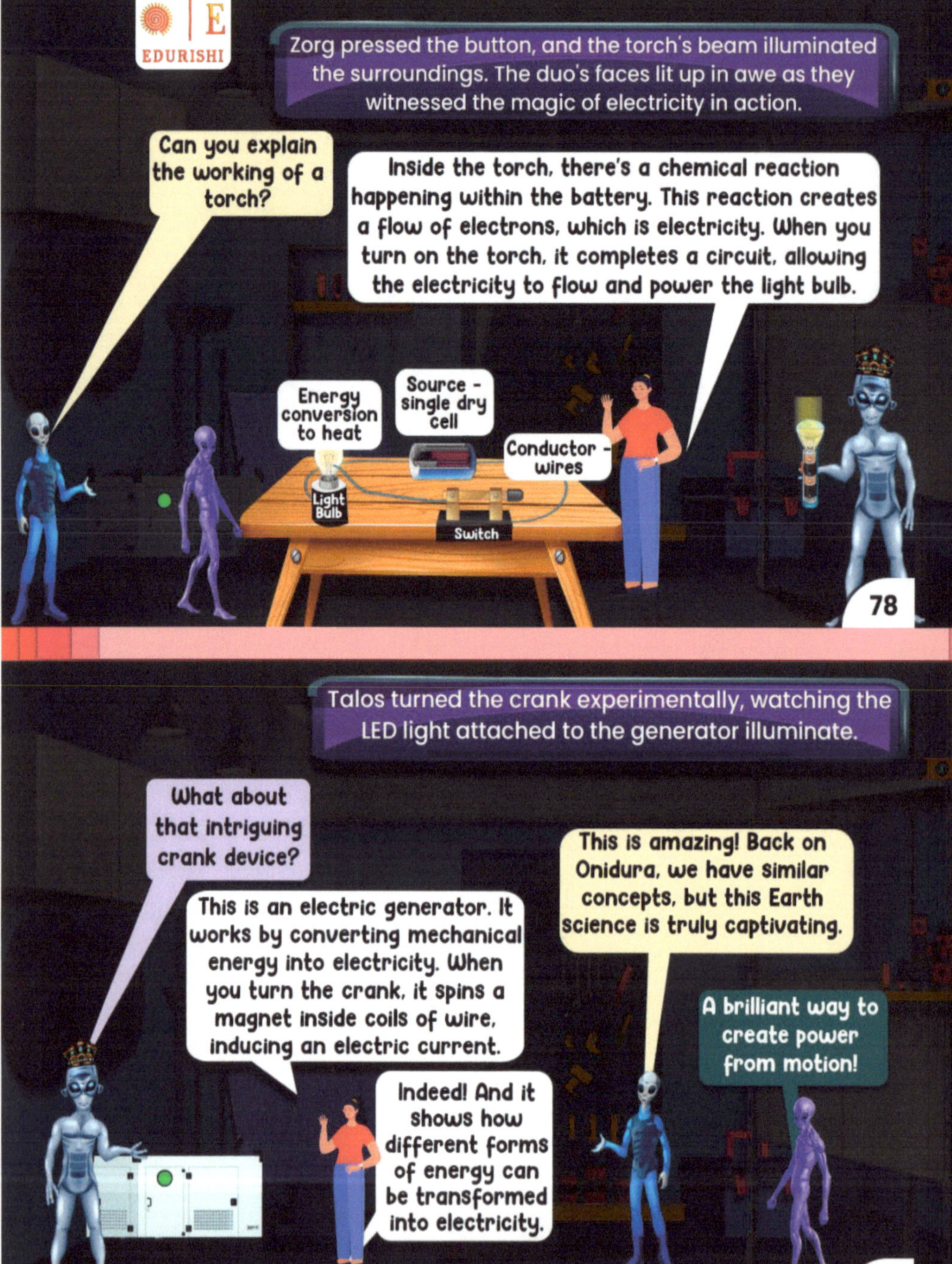

EDURISHI
Zorg pressed the button, and the torch's beam illuminated the surroundings. The duo's faces lit up in awe as they witnessed the magic of electricity in action.
Can you explain the working of a torch?
Inside the torch, there's a chemical reaction happening within the battery. This reaction creates a flow of electrons, which is electricity. When you turn on the torch, it completes a circuit, allowing the electricity to flow and power the light bulb.
Energy conversion to heat
Source - single dry cell
Conductor - wires
Light Bulb
Switch
78
Talos turned the crank experimentally, watching the LED light attached to the generator illuminate.
What about that intriguing crank device?
This is amazing! Back on Onidura, we have similar concepts, but this Earth science is truly captivating.
This is an electric generator. It works by converting mechanical energy into electricity. When you turn the crank, it spins a magnet inside coils of wire, inducing an electric current.
A brilliant way to create power from motion!
Indeed! And it shows how different forms of energy can be transformed into electricity.
79
41

And what about sustainable sources?
That's where solar panels come in. They harness the sun's energy to generate electricity.
See this solar panel? It's made up of solar cells that capture sunlight and convert it into electricity.
Do you use them in your house?
Come outside I will show you.
80
These are the solar panels which harness Sun's energy to produce electricity.
Sun's energy?
"Yes! Solar energy is harnessed from the sun's rays. Sunlight contains tiny particles called photons, and these photons can be captured by solar panels to generate electricity."
How does that panel captures Solar energy?
"The solar panel is made up of many solar cells. Each cell is made of silicon, a material that can convert sunlight into electricity."
81

This energy can be stored in battery for use when the Sun isn't shining.
Ah, like the torch powered by the batteries you showed us earlier?
Quite a remarkable way to gather energy.
Exactly the torch uses a battery to store energy. When you turn it on, the battery releases stored electricity, which powers the light.
82
But what exactly is this Electricity?
Imagine, a world of tiny particles called electrons. When these electrons flow through a conductor, they give rise to what we call electric current.
It seems creating electric current is like orchestrating a dance of electrons.
Are there any other uses of electricity apart from producing light?
Yes, electricity is used to power everything you see around us. It doesn't only produce light, it has heating and magnetic effects too.
83
43

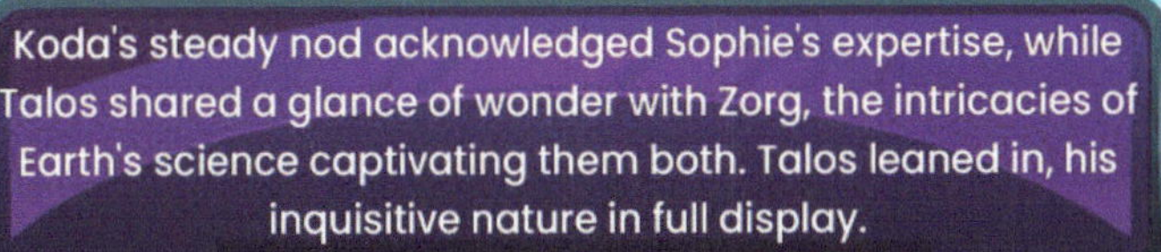

Koda's steady nod acknowledged Sophie's expertise, while Talos shared a glance of wonder with Zorg, the intricacies of Earth's science captivating them both. Talos leaned in, his inquisitive nature in full display.
EDURISHI
Now lets unveil the heating effect of electric current. As these electrons journey through a conductor, they collide with atoms, generating heat. This concept is the foundation of devices like heaters and stovetops.
So, it's like the electron's movement generates warmth?
Yes, come inside the house where I can show you these effects and devices.
84

The journey continued to the kitchen, a space filled with the aroma of a simmering soup. Sophie's gaze settled on the toaster and stovetop. She activated the toaster, showing the red-hot wires that toasted bread .
Now, let's explore the heating effect of electric current.
Why do the wires get hot?
So, it's like a dance of electrons creating warmth?
As electrons move through the wires, they generate heat, making our appliances functional.
Exactly! The dance of electrons within the wires which generate heat is what brings these appliances like electric heaters, toasters, and water heaters to life.
85

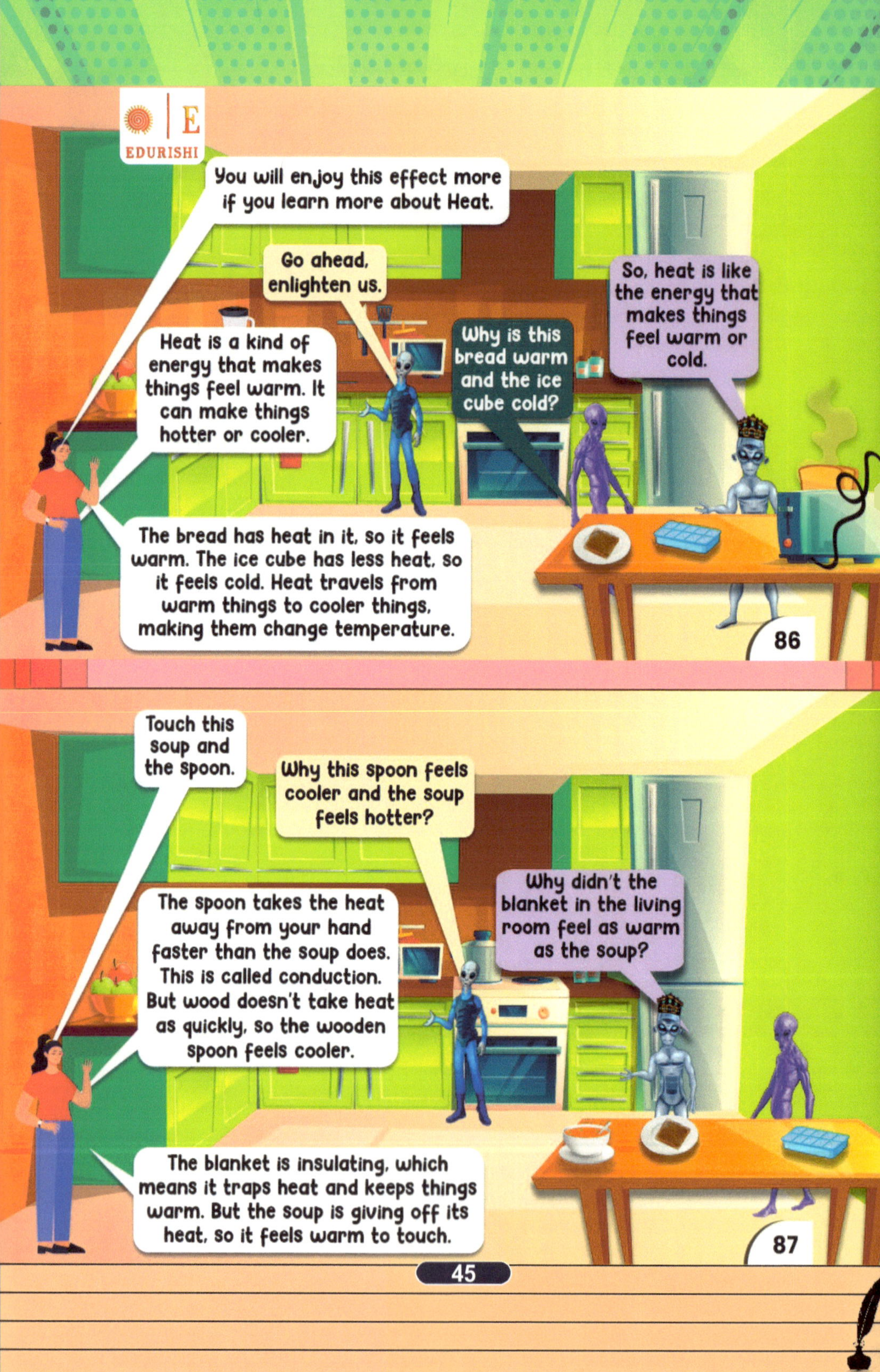

You will enjoy this effect more if you learn more about Heat.
Go ahead, enlighten us.
Why is this bread warm and the ice cube cold?
So, heat is like the energy that makes things feel warm or cold.
Heat is a kind of energy that makes things feel warm. It can make things hotter or cooler.
The bread has heat in it, so it feels warm. The ice cube has less heat, so it feels cold. Heat travels from warm things to cooler things, making them change temperature.
86
Touch this soup and the spoon.
Why this spoon feels cooler and the soup feels hotter?
Why didn't the blanket in the living room feel as warm as the soup?
The spoon takes the heat away from your hand faster than the soup does. This is called conduction. But wood doesn't take heat as quickly, so the wooden spoon feels cooler.
The blanket is insulating, which means it traps heat and keeps things warm. But the soup is giving off its heat, so it feels warm to touch.
87

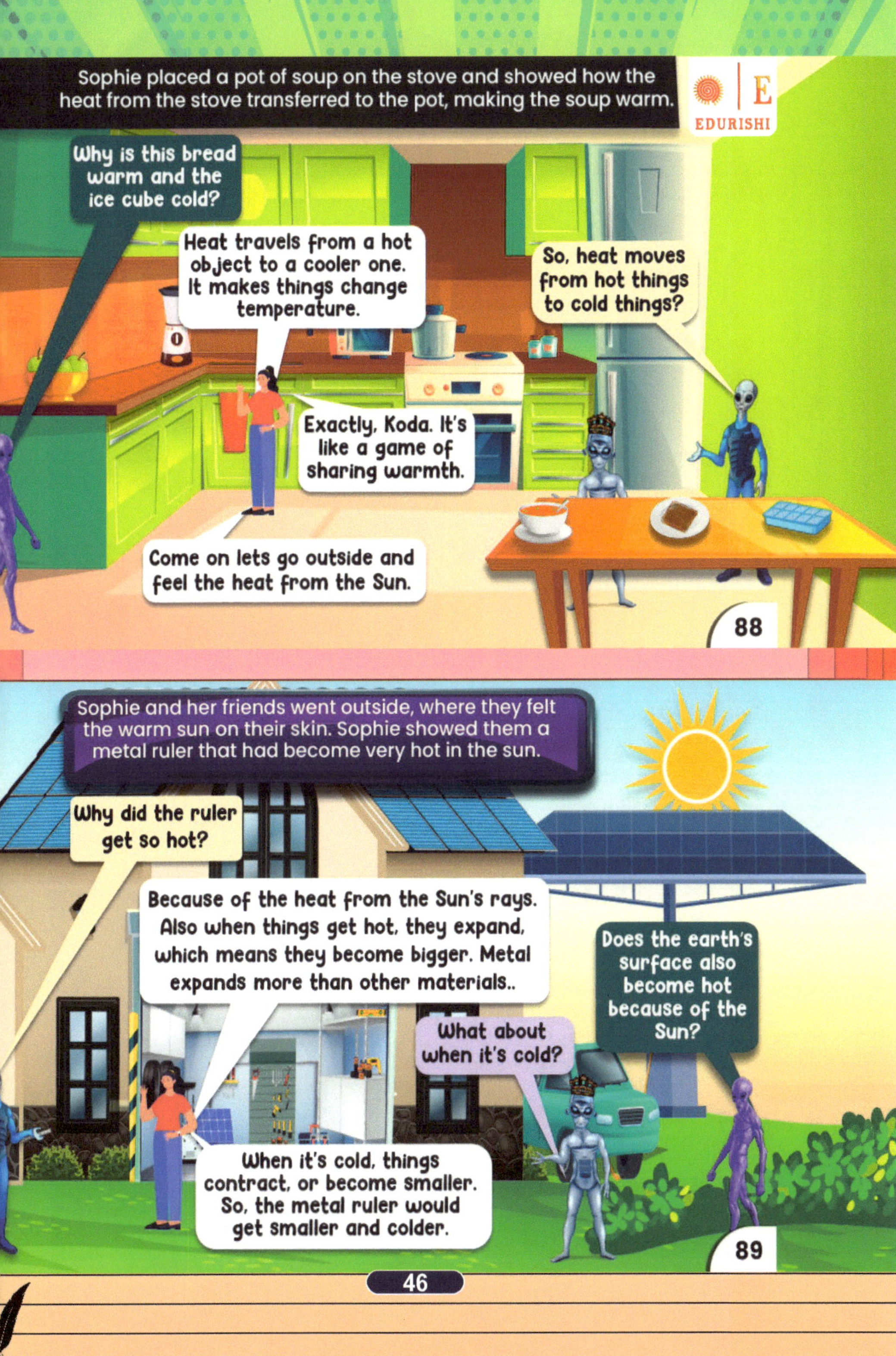
Sophie placed a pot of soup on the stove and showed how the heat from the stove transferred to the pot, making the soup warm.
EDURISHI
Why is this bread warm and the ice cube cold?
Heat travels from a hot object to a cooler one. It makes things change temperature.
So, heat moves from hot things to cold things?
Exactly, Koda. It's like a game of sharing warmth.
Come on lets go outside and feel the heat from the Sun.
88
Sophie and her friends went outside, where they felt the warm sun on their skin. Sophie showed them a metal ruler that had become very hot in the sun.
Why did the ruler get so hot?
Because of the heat from the Sun's rays. Also when things get hot, they expand, which means they become bigger. Metal expands more than other materials..
Does the earth's surface also become hot because of the Sun?
What about when it's cold?
When it's cold, things contract, or become smaller. So, the metal ruler would get smaller and colder.
89

EDURISHI
DAY TIME
NIGHT TIME
Let me show you..
90
Yes even Earth's surface gets hot but during the day, the land gets hotter faster than the sea. The warm air over the land rises, and cooler air from the sea moves in, creating a sea breeze.
What about at night?
At night, the land cools down faster. The cooler air above the land moves towards the warmer sea, creating a land breeze.
This is very useful.
Ok, lets go back inside as it is getting hotter and also I want to show you something.
91
47

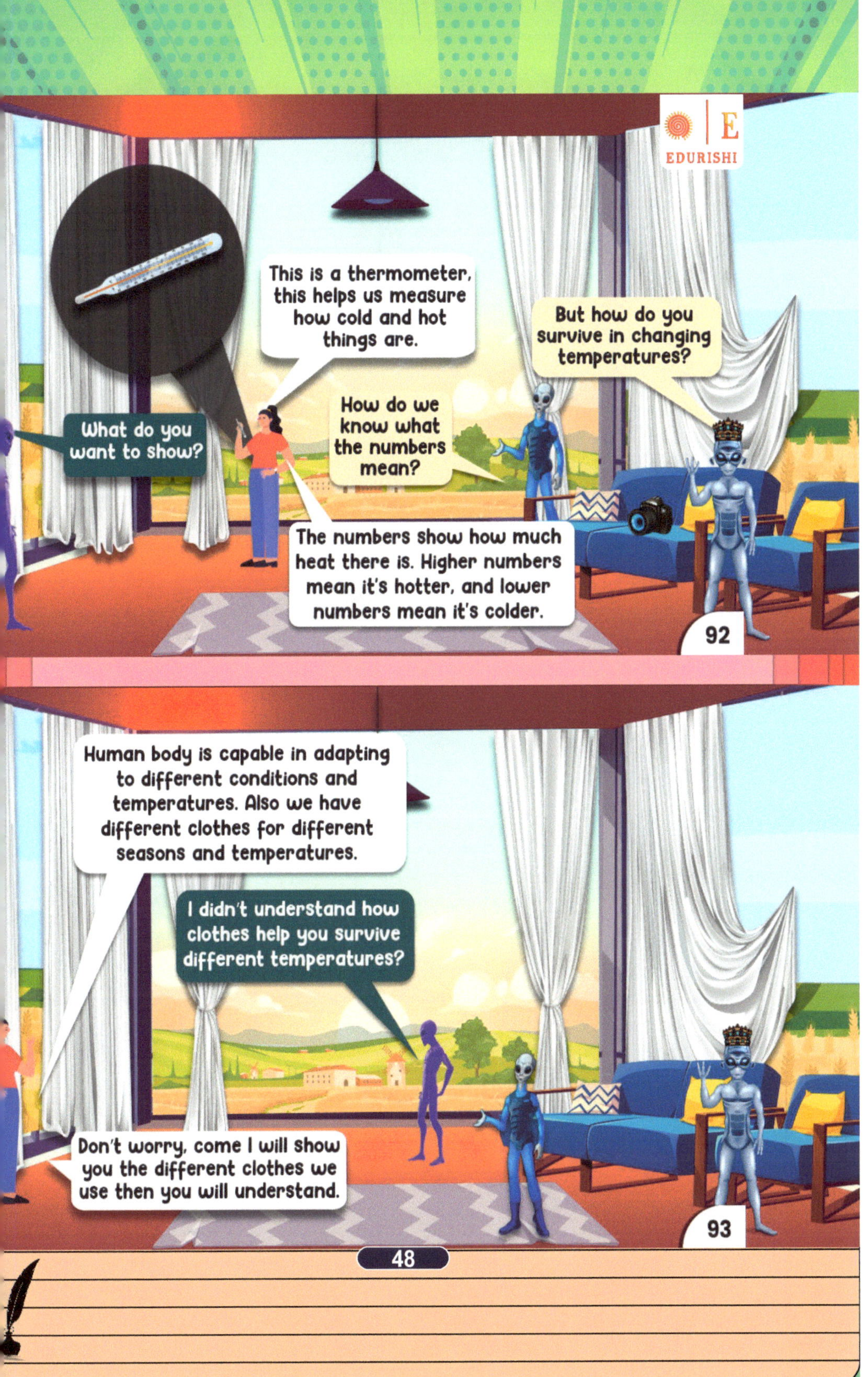
This is a thermometer, this helps us measure how cold and hot things are.
But how do you survive in changing temperatures?
What do you want to show?
How do we know what the numbers mean?
The numbers show how much heat there is. Higher numbers mean it's hotter, and lower numbers mean it's colder.
92
Human body is capable in adapting to different conditions and temperatures. Also we have different clothes for different seasons and temperatures.
I didn't understand how clothes help you survive different temperatures?
Don't worry, come I will show you the different clothes we use then you will understand.
93
EDURISHI

These are the kinds clothes which we use on Earth and we have different clothes for different seasons.
Why do you wear different clothes in different seasons?
Good question, Talos! When it's hot, like in summer, we wear light and cool clothes, like T-shirts and shorts. They help our body breathe and stay comfy.
What about when it's cold?
In cold seasons, like winter, we wear cozy and warm clothes, like sweaters and jackets. These clothes trap our body heat and keep us snug.
94
So, it's like choosing clothes that match the weather outside.
Scan for Electricity is energy Video
Exactly, Koda! Just like how we use thermometers to know how hot or cold it is, we choose clothes that help us feel just right in the different temperatures.
Wonderful, let's move to another realm of this dance.
Of course, lets go back to the garage where I can show you the magnetic effects of electricity.
95
49

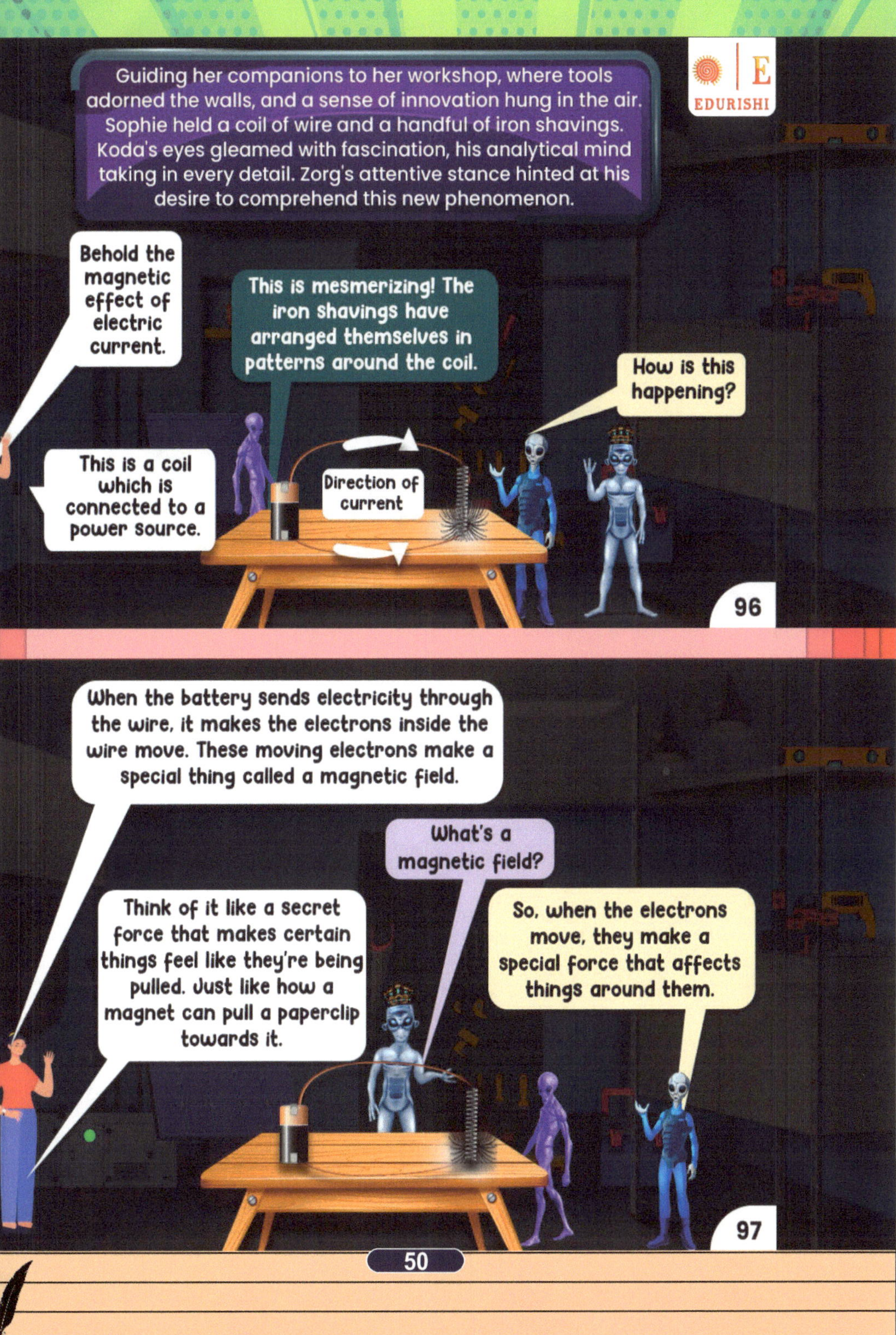

Guiding her companions to her workshop, where tools adorned the walls, and a sense of innovation hung in the air. Sophie held a coil of wire and a handful of iron shavings. Koda's eyes gleamed with fascination, his analytical mind taking in every detail. Zorg's attentive stance hinted at his desire to comprehend this new phenomenon.
Behold the magnetic effect of electric current.
This is mesmerizing! The iron shavings have arranged themselves in patterns around the coil.
How is this happening?
This is a coil which is connected to a power source.
Direction of current
96
When the battery sends electricity through the wire, it makes the electrons inside the wire move. These moving electrons make a special thing called a magnetic field.
What's a magnetic field?
Think of it like a secret force that makes certain things feel like they're being pulled. Just like how a magnet can pull a paperclip towards it.
So, when the electrons move, they make a special force that affects things around them.
97
50

Exactly! And we can use this special force to do many helpful things. In real life, we use this to make things like powerful cranes, super-fast trains, and even machines that help doctors see inside our bodies.
So, by making electricity flow, we can make things act like magnets?
That's right, Talos! It's like magic science that helps us make our world better.
Can you show us these.
98
Magnetism? What's that all about?
I'm eager to learn about these mysterious magnets.
Let's begin by talking about magnets and how they work. Imagine this old toolbox as our first stop.
Inside this toolbox, I have two magnets. They attract certain types of metal, like iron. When I bring the magnets close to this paperclip, watch what happens.
S N N S
99
51
EDURISHI

The paperclip is sticking to the magnets!
That's right, Talos! Magnets have invisible forces that pull certain materials towards them. This force is called magnetism. Now, let's talk about the poles of a magnet. Just like Earth has a North Pole and a South Pole, magnets have their own poles. Let's use these bar magnets to see.
One end of the magnet is attracting, while the other end isn't doing anything!
N S N S
100
Exactly, Zorg! The end that points towards the Earth's North Pole is the north-seeking pole of the magnet, while the other end is the south-seeking pole. Now, watch closely as I bring these two north poles of the magnets together.
They're pushing each other away!
Yes, Koda! Like poles of magnets repel, or push away, each other. Now, if I bring the north pole of one magnet close to the south pole of another.
N S S N
101

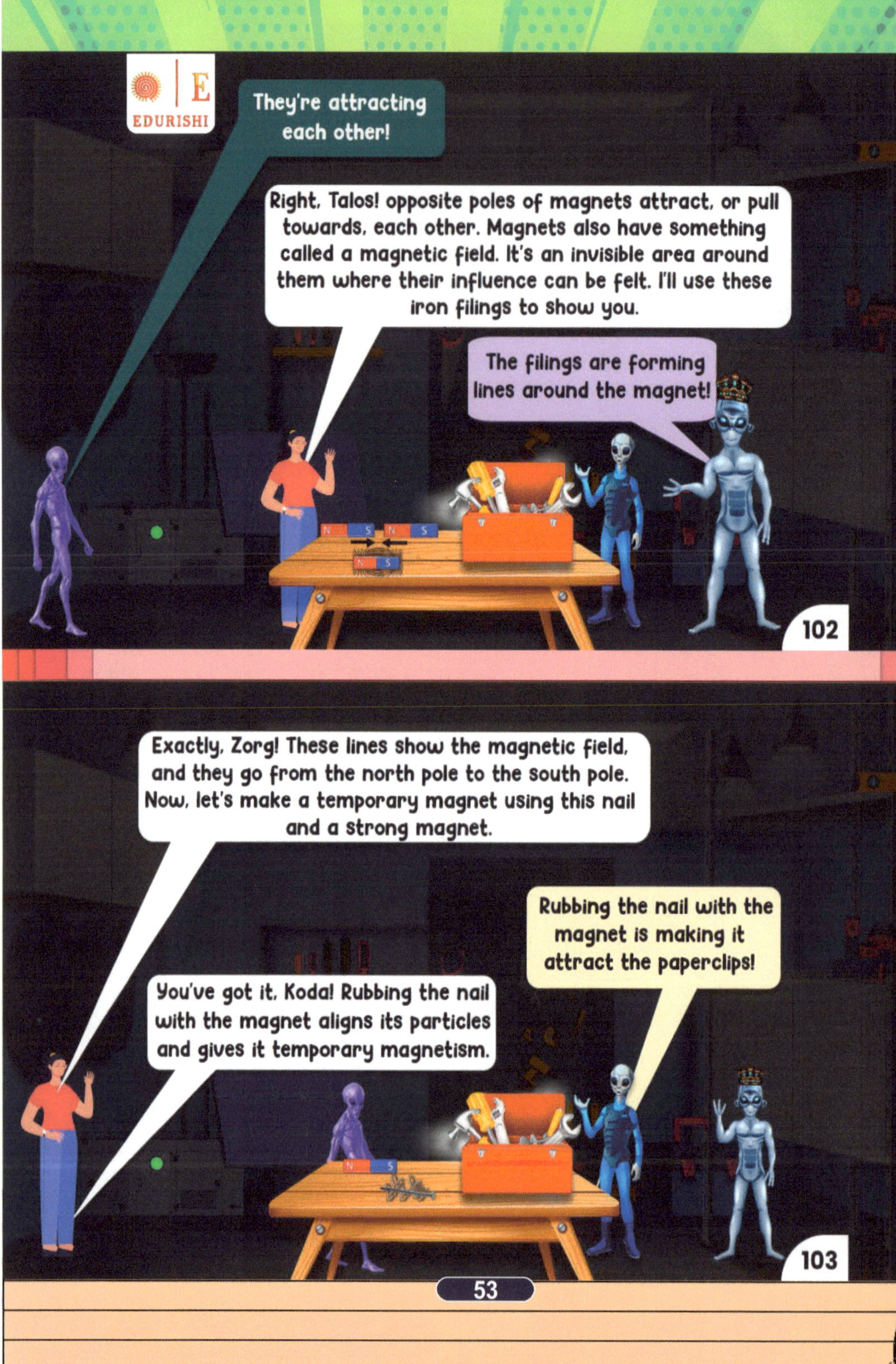
EDURISHI
They're attracting each other!
Right, Talos! opposite poles of magnets attract, or pull towards, each other. Magnets also have something called a magnetic field. It's an invisible area around them where their influence can be felt. I'll use these iron filings to show you.
The filings are forming lines around the magnet!
N S S N
N S
102
Exactly, Zorg! These lines show the magnetic field, and they go from the north pole to the south pole. Now, let's make a temporary magnet using this nail and a strong magnet.
Rubbing the nail with the magnet is making it attract the paperclips!
You've got it, Koda! Rubbing the nail with the magnet aligns its particles and gives it temporary magnetism.
N S
103

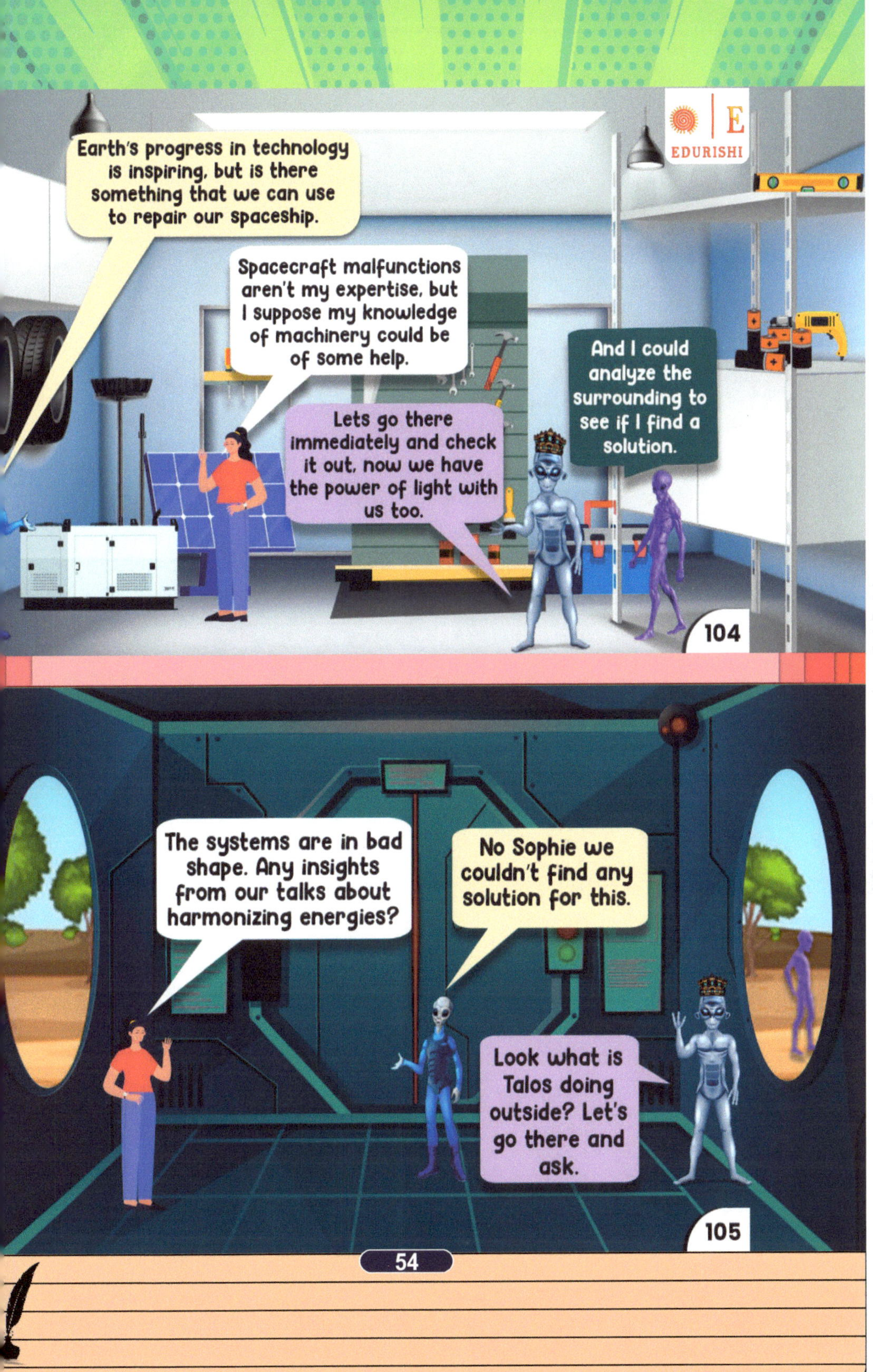

Earth's progress in technology is inspiring, but is there something that we can use to repair our spaceship.
Spacecraft malfunctions aren't my expertise, but I suppose my knowledge of machinery could be of some help.
Lets go there immediately and check it out, now we have the power of light with us too.
And I could analyze the surrounding to see if I find a solution.
104
The systems are in bad shape. Any insights from our talks about harmonizing energies?
No Sophie we couldn't find any solution for this.
Look what is Talos doing outside? Let's go there and ask.
105
54

What are you doing here Talos?
I have always wondered, how are all these plants so different from each other? What makes them unique?
Talos, I might have an answer for you.
Talos, that's a great question. Plants are indeed incredibly diverse. Anahita, can you share your insight?
Of course, Sophie. Each plant has its own form and function that makes it distinct. Take me, for example. I'm a water lily flower, suited for life in a pond.
106
Anahita, you're not like the other plants. What sets you apart?
Well, Talos that's where understanding the different types of plants comes in.
How you can differentiate them?
There are herbs, like basil and mint, that are small and often used in cooking. Then there are shrubs – medium-sized plants with woody stems. And the towering trees that provide shade and shelter.
107
55

So, it's about their sizes and roles?
How about we take a walk to my garden? I can show you live examples of these plant types and more.
Exactly, Zorg! And don't forget about creepers that spread along the ground, and climbers that use structures to reach great heights.
Creepers and climbers, got it!
Lead the way, Sophie.
108
They all reach Sophie's vibrant garden.
Here we are, a place filled with the wonders of plants.
Where do these plants come from?
I was going to tell you this. Let's start with the germination process. You see these pots with sprouting seedlings?
Those tiny plants are just starting out!
109

Exactly, Talos. These are baby plants. They begin as seeds, and when they germinate, a root pushes into the soil for nutrients, while a shoot reaches up for sunlight.
Whoa, there it is! It's like the plant's first step into the world!
As the shoot continues to grow, it'll eventually develop leaves, and the baby plant will start looking more like a proper plant.
EDURISHI
110
Oh, look at these lovely flowers in Sophie's garden.
Flowers? They're not just pretty things?
Yeah, what's so special about them?
They have different parts, each with its own role.
111
57

Flower has a colorful stage. Look at this flower the outermost part is the sepal. It's like the curtain that protects the flower before it blooms.
As the curtain opens, you'll see the petals. These are the colorful, delicate parts that attract pollinators like bees and butterflies.
Sepal? I've never heard of that.
No worries, Zorg! Just think of it as the flower's bodyguard.
Petals are like the flower's invitation card, right?
SEPAL
PETAL
112
Exactly, Talos! Now, let's go deeper. You'll find the stamen, the male part. It's like the pollen factory, producing tiny grains that help in making seeds.
Stamen, pollen... this is new!
Now, right in the center is the pistil, the female part. It has the stigma, where pollen lands, the style, like a bridge, and the ovary, where seeds develop.
Pollen grains are like plant dust, Koda. They're carried by the wind or pollinators to other flowers.
STAMEN
STIGMA
So, the flower's not just about looks, it's about life too!
113
EDURISHI

You've got it, Talos! When the pollen meets the ovary, magic happens, and seeds are created.
This is like a flower's secret life!
Now that we've uncovered the secrets of flowers, how about we venture underground and explore the fascinating world of roots?
OVARY
114
Sophie's garden, where Anahita, Sophie, Talos, Zorg, and Koda are gathered around a patch of plants with various root forms.
Hey everyone, check out these plants in my garden! They all have different types of roots that help them grow strong and healthy.
That's right, Sophie. Roots are like a plant's underground support system. Let me explain a bit more about them.
Please do, Anahita!
Okay, let's start with the fibrous roots. Fibrous roots are horizontal and wide spreading with only a few roots that go deep vertically downward.
115

EDURISHI

Ah, so those are fibrous roots. Got it.
And over here, we have this sunflower with a taproot. Look how it goes deep down into the ground. Taproots are like anchors that keep the plant steady and help it reach water deep below the surface.
So, taproots go deep, while fibrous roots spread out.
I'm sorry to interrupt, everyone, but I must go back to my pond.
Alright, Anahita.
116

Sophie's garden, a little while later. The group is now near a variety of plants with different types of stems.
You know, while we were talking about roots earlier, it got me wondering about the parts of plants above the ground.
Great question, Talos! Stems are like the highways that connect different parts of the plant.
Oh, are there different types of stems like there are different types of roots?
Absolutely, Koda! Take a look at this bamboo. It has a culm, which is a type of stem that's hollow and sturdy. It helps the bamboo stand tall.
117

And here we have this rose bush with thorns on its stems. Thorns are actually modified stems that help protect the plant from animals.
And what about those plant that are really spiky?
Those are actually spines on a cactus. The cactus has tiny leaves, but they've evolved into spines to help reduce water loss and protect the plant.
So, leaves can change their form to do different jobs!
yes Talos.
118
Okay, Sophie, we just saw a ton of plants, but there's so much we don't understand. Like, how do plants actually make more of themselves?
Plants have different modes of reproduction. Some reproduce with the help of seeds, while others use special methods.
But how do they do it? We've seen flowers and stuff, but is that where it all starts?
Plants have some interesting ways of reproducing. Let me break it down for you.
119
61

Well, have you ever heard of budding? Some plants can create new individuals by growing tiny versions of themselves on their own bodies.
Wait, they just sprout new plants from their own parts?
Exactly! And some plants reproduce through spore formation. They release tiny spores into the air, and when these spores land in the right spot, they can grow into new plants. Let's move to the kitchen were I can show you some examples of it.
Come on let's go inside.
EDURISHI
E
120
Look closely at these tiny structures on potato. Some plants reproduce through spore formation. Take a look over bread mould.
They look like small bumps on the potato's surface.
Exactly! And then there's something called fragmentation. Certain plants can break into pieces, and each piece can grow into a new plant. Lets go outside where I can show you process.
sure, Sophie.
Sporangium
Spores
BUDDING
SPORE FORMATION
121

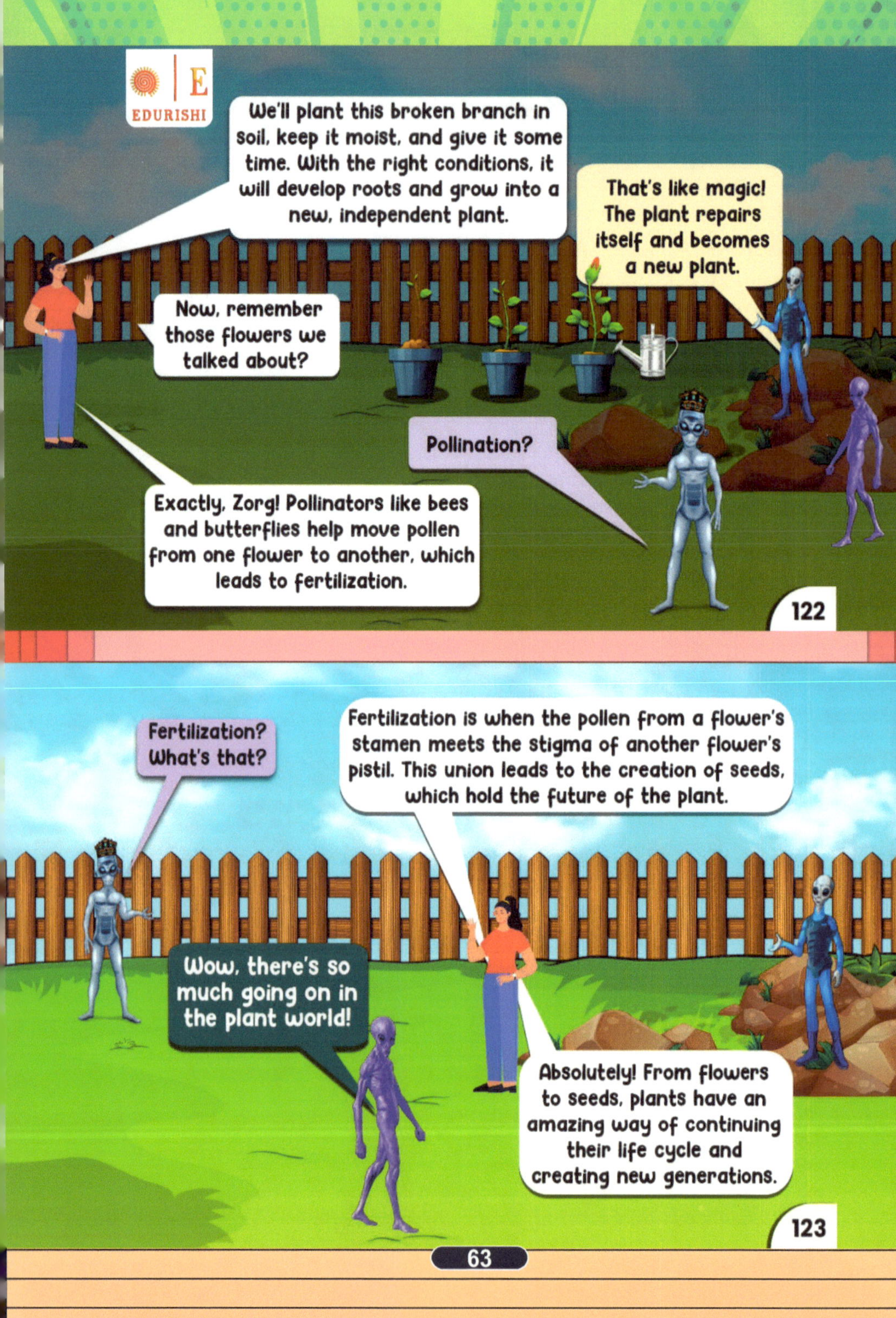

EDURISHI
We'll plant this broken branch in soil, keep it moist, and give it some time. With the right conditions, it will develop roots and grow into a new, independent plant.
That's like magic! The plant repairs itself and becomes a new plant.
Now, remember those flowers we talked about?
Pollination?
Exactly, Zorg! Pollinators like bees and butterflies help move pollen from one flower to another, which leads to fertilization.
122
Fertilization? What's that?
Fertilization is when the pollen from a flower's stamen meets the stigma of another flower's pistil. This union leads to the creation of seeds, which hold the future of the plant.
Wow, there's so much going on in the plant world!
Absolutely! From flowers to seeds, plants have an amazing way of continuing their life cycle and creating new generations.
123
63

A serene part of Sophie's garden, with various types of plants around, showcasing their modes of nutrition. The group is gathered, curious to learn more about plant nutrition.

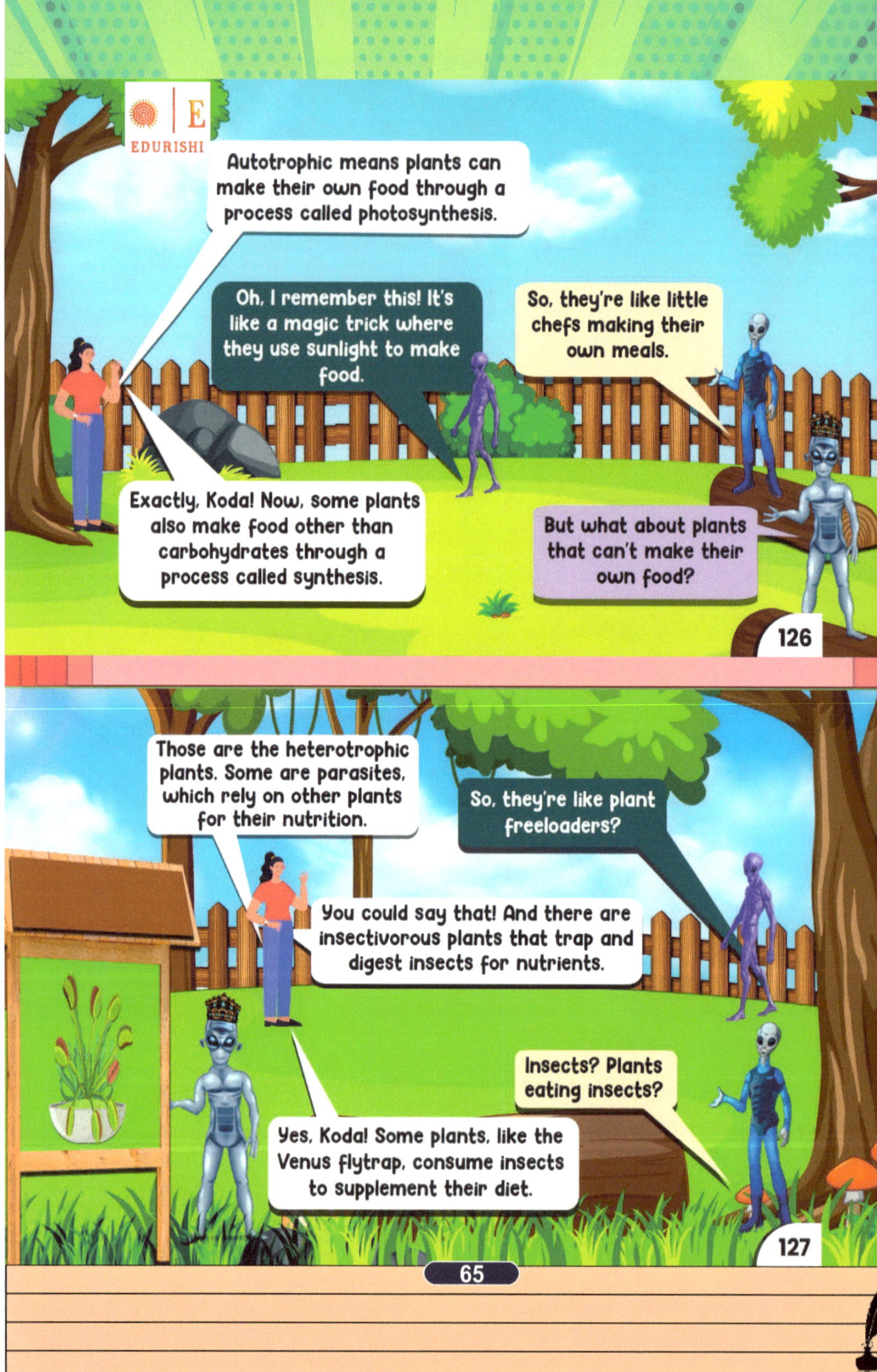

Autotrophic means plants can make their own food through a process called photosynthesis.
Oh, I remember this! It's like a magic trick where they use sunlight to make food.
So, they're like little chefs making their own meals.
Exactly, Koda! Now, some plants also make food other than carbohydrates through a process called synthesis.
But what about plants that can't make their own food?
126

Those are the heterotrophic plants. Some are parasites, which rely on other plants for their nutrition.
So, they're like plant freeloaders?
You could say that! And there are insectivorous plants that trap and digest insects for nutrients.
Insects? Plants eating insects?
Yes, Koda! Some plants, like the Venus flytrap, consume insects to supplement their diet.
127

what about this mushrooms ? They falls in which category?
Fungi, like mushrooms, are saprotrophs. They break down dead organic matter and absorb the nutrients.
So, they're like nature's recyclers.
Precisely, Koda ! And speaking of nutrients, plants also play a role in replenishing the soil by shedding leaves.
128
After discussing plant forms and functions Sophie and her friends are walking through the farm, observing the animals with curiosity.
Wow, Sophie, your farm is full of animals! But I've got a million questions about them.
Wait, who's that talking?
Feel free to ask away!
A talking parrot? That's incredible!
Oh, that's Faby, my parrot friend. She's quite the chatterbox.
129

Well, you're in luck. I may not know everything, but I can certainly help with a lot of animal related questions. Fire away!
Alright, Faby, I've got a question that's been bugging me for a while. How do cows even stand on their legs? They're so big!
So, animals have bones too?
Great observation, Koda! Their legs are made up of bones, cartilage, and ligaments that provide support for their heavy bodies.
130
Absolutely, Zorg! Animals have skeletal systems that give them shape and structure. But they also have other incredible adaptations.
But how do animals with multiple legs move?
Those animals have specialized structures too. Look that spider have jointed legs so that they can move in various ways.
I'm eager to learn about animal joints.
Alright Koda then let's move ahead to the lab.
131
EDURISHI
67

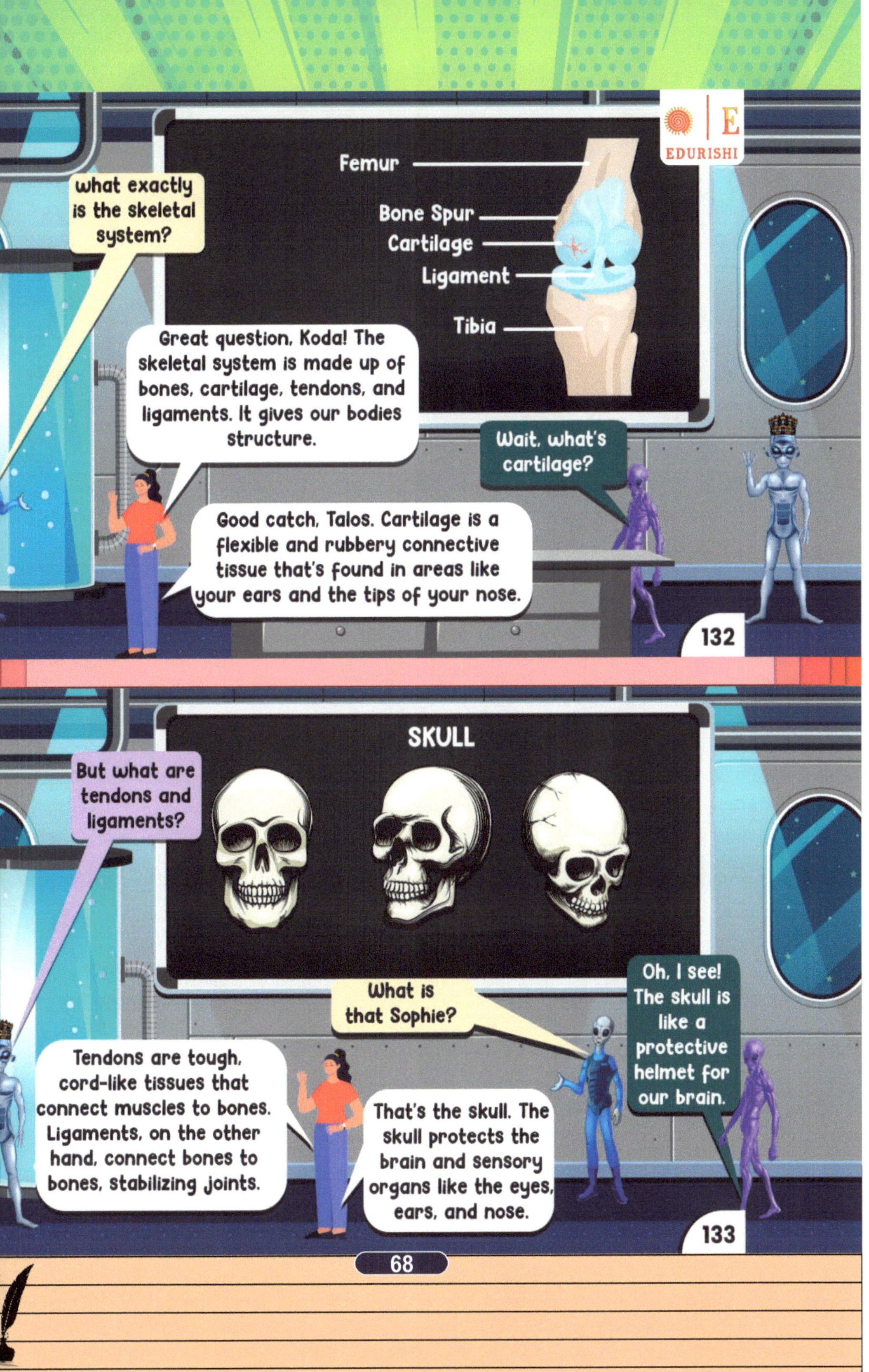

Femur
Bone Spur
Cartilage
Ligament
Tibia
what exactly is the skeletal system?
Great question, Koda! The skeletal system is made up of bones, cartilage, tendons, and ligaments. It gives our bodies structure.
Wait, what's cartilage?
Good catch, Talos. Cartilage is a flexible and rubbery connective tissue that's found in areas like your ears and the tips of your nose.
132
SKULL
But what are tendons and ligaments?
What is that Sophie?
Oh, I see! The skull is like a protective helmet for our brain.
Tendons are tough, cord-like tissues that connect muscles to bones. Ligaments, on the other hand, connect bones to bones, stabilizing joints.
That's the skull. The skull protects the brain and sensory organs like the eyes, ears, and nose.
133
68

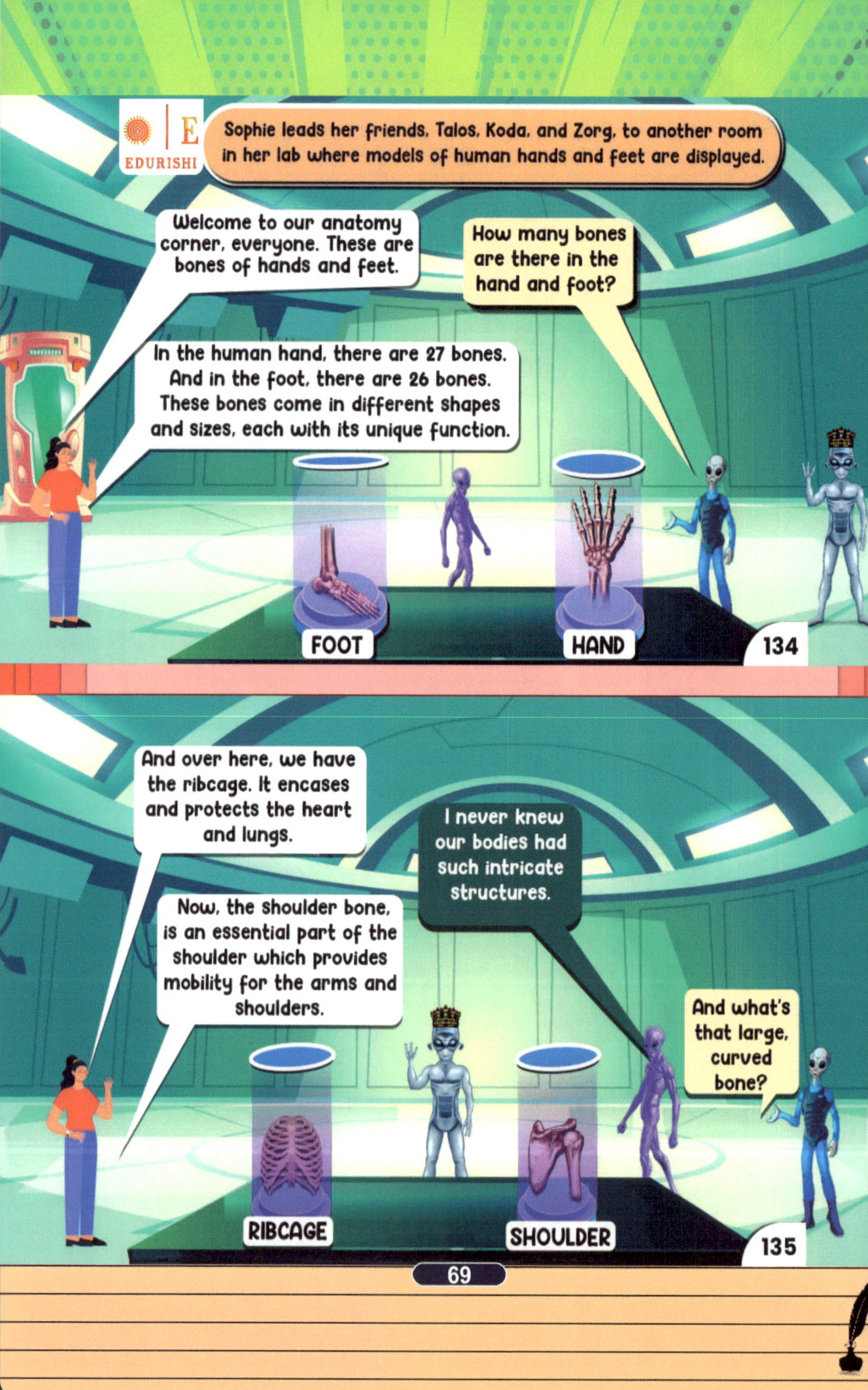
Sophie leads her friends, Talos, Koda, and Zorg, to another room in her lab where models of human hands and feet are displayed.
Welcome to our anatomy corner, everyone. These are bones of hands and feet.
How many bones are there in the hand and foot?
In the human hand, there are 27 bones. And in the foot, there are 26 bones. These bones come in different shapes and sizes, each with its unique function.
FOOT
HAND
134
And over here, we have the ribcage. It encases and protects the heart and lungs.
I never knew our bodies had such intricate structures.
Now, the shoulder bone, is an essential part of the shoulder which provides mobility for the arms and shoulders.
And what's that large, curved bone?
RIBCAGE
SHOULDER
135
69

EDURISHI

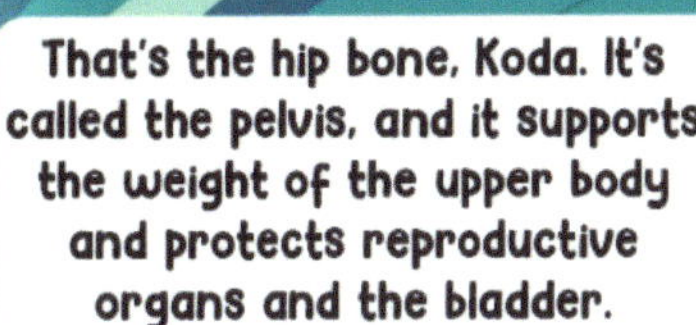

That's the hip bone, Koda. It's called the pelvis, and it supports the weight of the upper body and protects reproductive organs and the bladder.
I've been thinking about something. You know how animals move differently, right? How come they're so different?
Great question, Talos. You're onto something important. How about we take a trip to the nearby zoo? I think it might help you understand this better.
That sounds fun! Let's head towards zoo.
HIP BONE
136

ZOO
Whoa, look at these bones! They're huge! What kind of animals did these belong to?
These are the fossils of ancient creatures that once roamed the Earth.
Sophie, why do some animals have different structures?
Animals have adapted their front and back structures based on how they move and what they need to do.
I can't believe these bones are so old!
137

ZOO
EDURISHI
Look at these joints! They look so intricate. What do they do?
Joints are like the hinges that allow movement in our bodies..
So, animals with different types of joints move in different ways?
You got it, Talos! Just like humans, animals movement abilities are closely tied to the kinds of joints they have.
138
Look at all these animals! They're so different from each other.
Yes Talos! This is because each animal is different from other. Look at this birds. Their wings are designed for flying, so they can soar through the air and cover great distances.
But how do they all move in their own unique ways?
139
71

And what about that animal which is so graceful in the water?
That's fish! They have streamlined bodies and fins that help them navigate through the water.
Wow, that's interesting! And what about that animal which is moving so differently?
That's Snake. They use their flexible bodies to slither on the ground. Their scales help them grip and push against the surface, allowing them to move forward.
140
what about that tiny creature which is moving slowly and didn't have legs at all!
Hey, Sophie, how come that giraffe eats leaves way up there? It's so different from how we eat.
That's the Snail. Snails move by gliding on a trail of mucus they produce.
It's amazing how each animal has found its own way to get around and survive.
Koda, you've got a keen eye! Animals do have unique ways of eating. Let's take a stroll to science lab, to learn more about it.
141

HUMAN DIGESTIVE SYSTEM
MOUTH
LIVER
ESOPHAGUS
STOMACH
SMALL INTESTINE
RECTUM
LARGE INTESTINE
Alright, everyone. Here, we can delve deeper into the world of nutrition in animals.
Well, humans eat food with their mouth, chew it with their teeth, and then their digestive system takes over.
But what exactly is nutrition?
Different ways? Like what?
Good question, Koda. Nutrition is all about how living organisms get the energy and nutrients. Let's start with the different ways animals take in food.
142
COW
What about tiny creature that eats in a really unconventional manner. They doesn't have a mouth or a stomach like we do.
And what about animals that eat grass or plants?
Grass-eating animals, like cows, have specialized stomachs with multiple chambers to help them digest tough plant material.
That's fascinating!
143
73

AMOEBA
Ah, great question, Talos! That is Amoeba. It feed through a process called phagocytosis, where they engulf tiny food particles and digest them within their cell.
We respire because our cells need oxygen to generate energy.
This is just one part of how organisms function. Another critical process is respiration. It's about how we get oxygen and release carbon dioxide.
So, why do we respire?
144
FISH
And what about other animals? Do they breathe the same way we do?
GILLS
gills what is that?
Well, many animals do breathe, but they have different sytems. Some use gills, while others have specialized adaptations for life in different environments.
some creatures can even breathe underwater like fish. They use gills to extract oxygen from water.
145

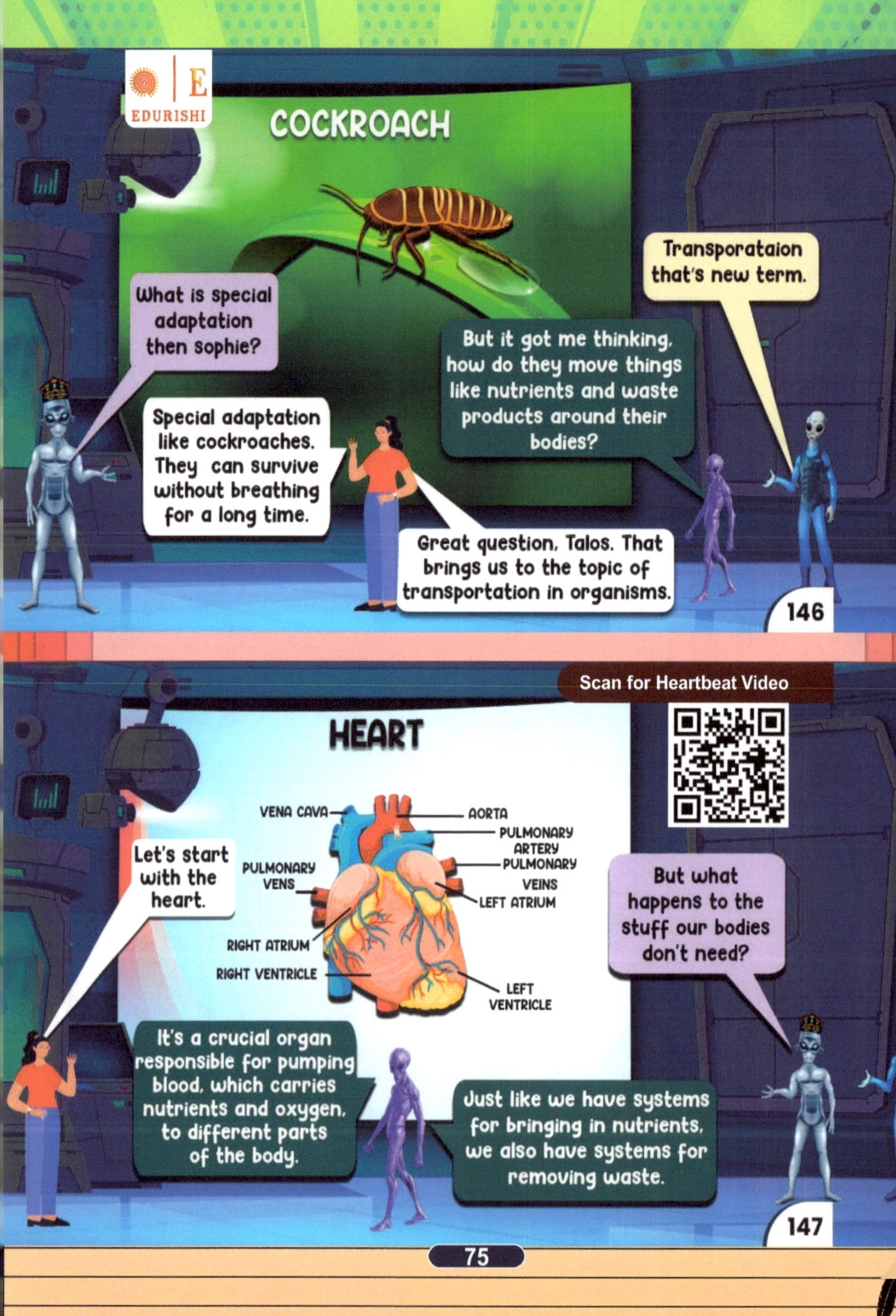
EDURISHI
COCKROACH
What is special adaptation then sophie?
Special adaptation like cockroaches. They can survive without breathing for a long time.
But it got me thinking, how do they move things like nutrients and waste products around their bodies?
Transportaion that's new term.
Great question, Talos. That brings us to the topic of transportation in organisms.
146
Scan for Heartbeat Video
HEART
VENA CAVA
AORTA
PULMONARY ARTERY
PULMONARY VEINS
LEFT ATRIUM
PULMONARY VENS
RIGHT ATRIUM
RIGHT VENTRICLE
LEFT VENTRICLE
Let's start with the heart.
But what happens to the stuff our bodies don't need?
It's a crucial organ responsible for pumping blood, which carries nutrients and oxygen, to different parts of the body.
Just like we have systems for bringing in nutrients, we also have systems for removing waste.
147
75

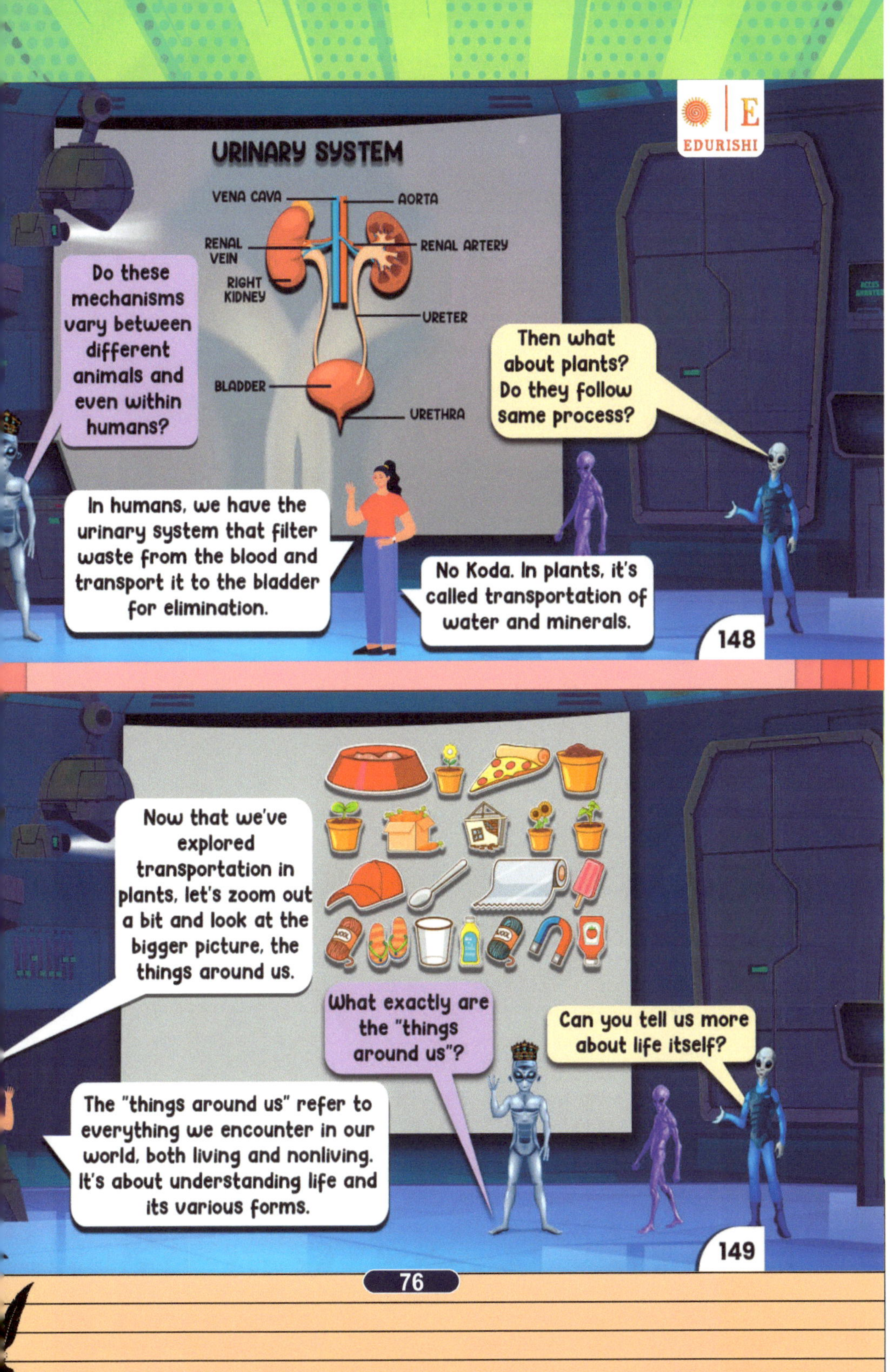
URINARY SYSTEM
VENA CAVA
AORTA
RENAL VEIN
RENAL ARTERY
RIGHT KIDNEY
URETER
BLADDER
URETHRA
EDURISHI
Do these mechanisms vary between different animals and even within humans?
Then what about plants? Do they follow same process?
In humans, we have the urinary system that filter waste from the blood and transport it to the bladder for elimination.
No Koda. In plants, it's called transportation of water and minerals.
148
Now that we've explored transportation in plants, let's zoom out a bit and look at the bigger picture, the things around us.
What exactly are the "things around us"?
Can you tell us more about life itself?
The "things around us" refer to everything we encounter in our world, both living and nonliving. It's about understanding life and its various forms.
149
76

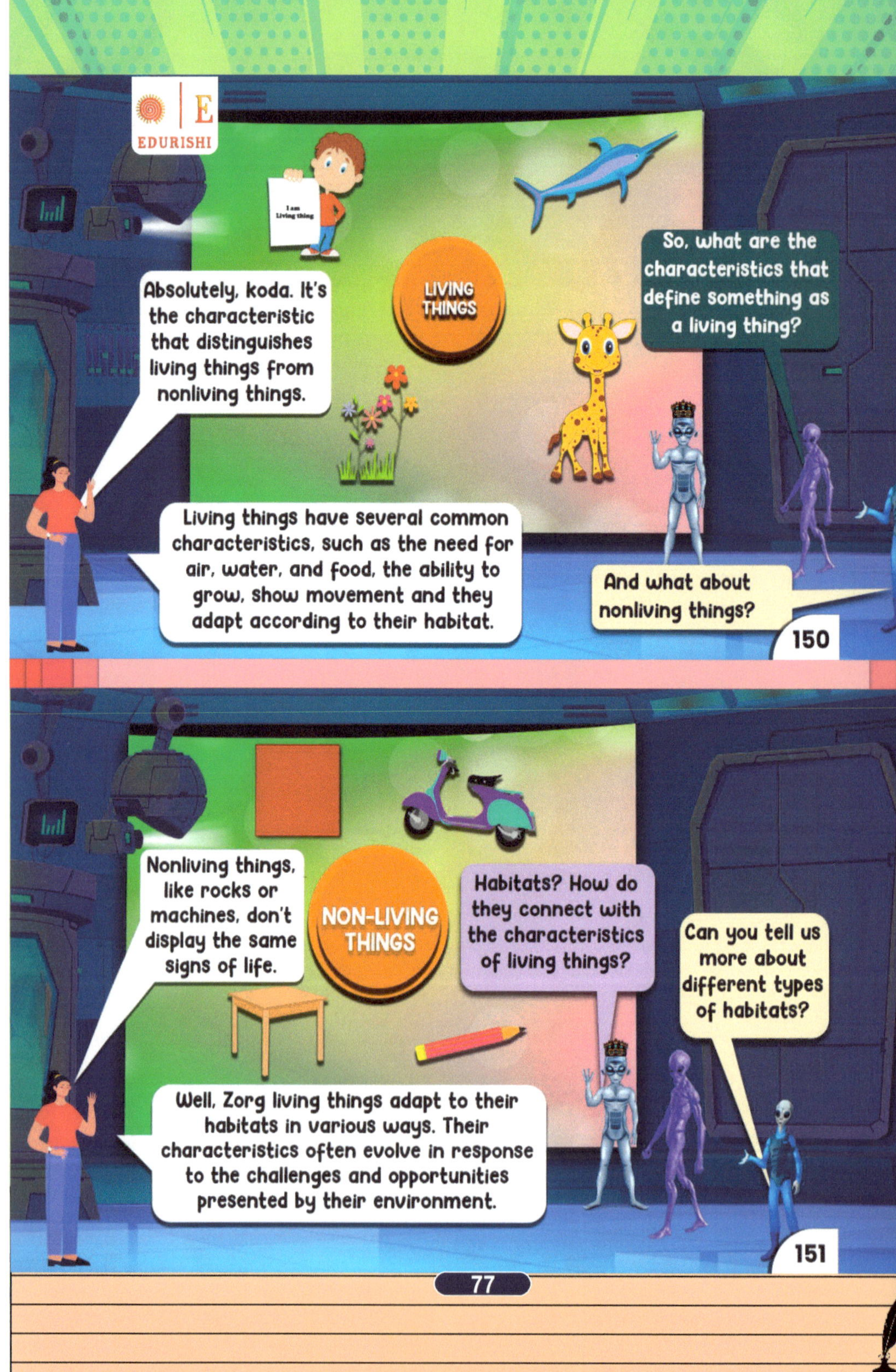
I am Living thing
LIVING THINGS
So, what are the characteristics that define something as a living thing?
Absolutely, koda. It's the characteristic that distinguishes living things from nonliving things.
Living things have several common characteristics, such as the need for air, water, and food, the ability to grow, show movement and they adapt according to their habitat.
And what about nonliving things?
150
Nonliving things, like rocks or machines, don't display the same signs of life.
NON-LIVING THINGS
Habitats? How do they connect with the characteristics of living things?
Can you tell us more about different types of habitats?
Well, Zorg living things adapt to their habitats in various ways. Their characteristics often evolve in response to the challenges and opportunities presented by their environment.
151
77

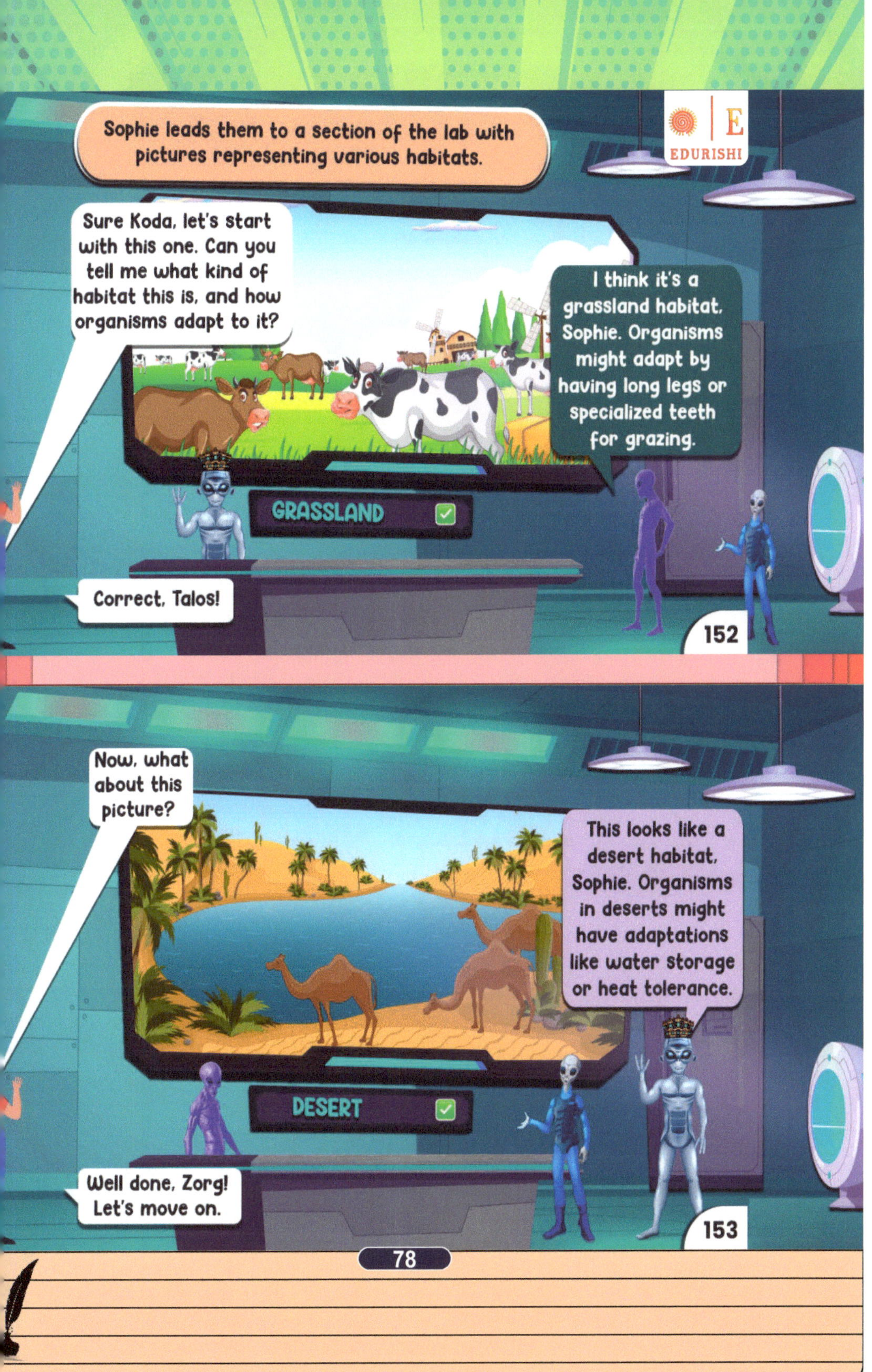

Sophie leads them to a section of the lab with pictures representing various habitats.
Sure Koda, let's start with this one. Can you tell me what kind of habitat this is, and how organisms adapt to it?
I think it's a grassland habitat, Sophie. Organisms might adapt by having long legs or specialized teeth for grazing.
GRASSLAND
Correct, Talos!
152
Now, what about this picture?
This looks like a desert habitat, Sophie. Organisms in deserts might have adaptations like water storage or heat tolerance.
DESERT
Well done, Zorg! Let's move on.
153
78
EDURISHI

Can you describe the animals found living in this harsh environment?
It seems like we're looking at the Arctic or a snow-covered polar region. Animals here might have thick fur or blubber for insulation.
POLAR REGION
Well done, Koda! You've all made some great connections between habitats and adaptations.
154
Sophie and her friends, Zorg, Talos, and Koda, are in the garden area, concluding their discussion about adaptation and habitats.
Adaptation and habitats are truly fascinating topics. But now, you've got me curious about something else.
What's on your mind, Zorg?
Well, I've been thinking about the incredible places where living things adapt, it's vast, green, and full of life.
Vast, green, full of life...?
155
79
EDURISHI

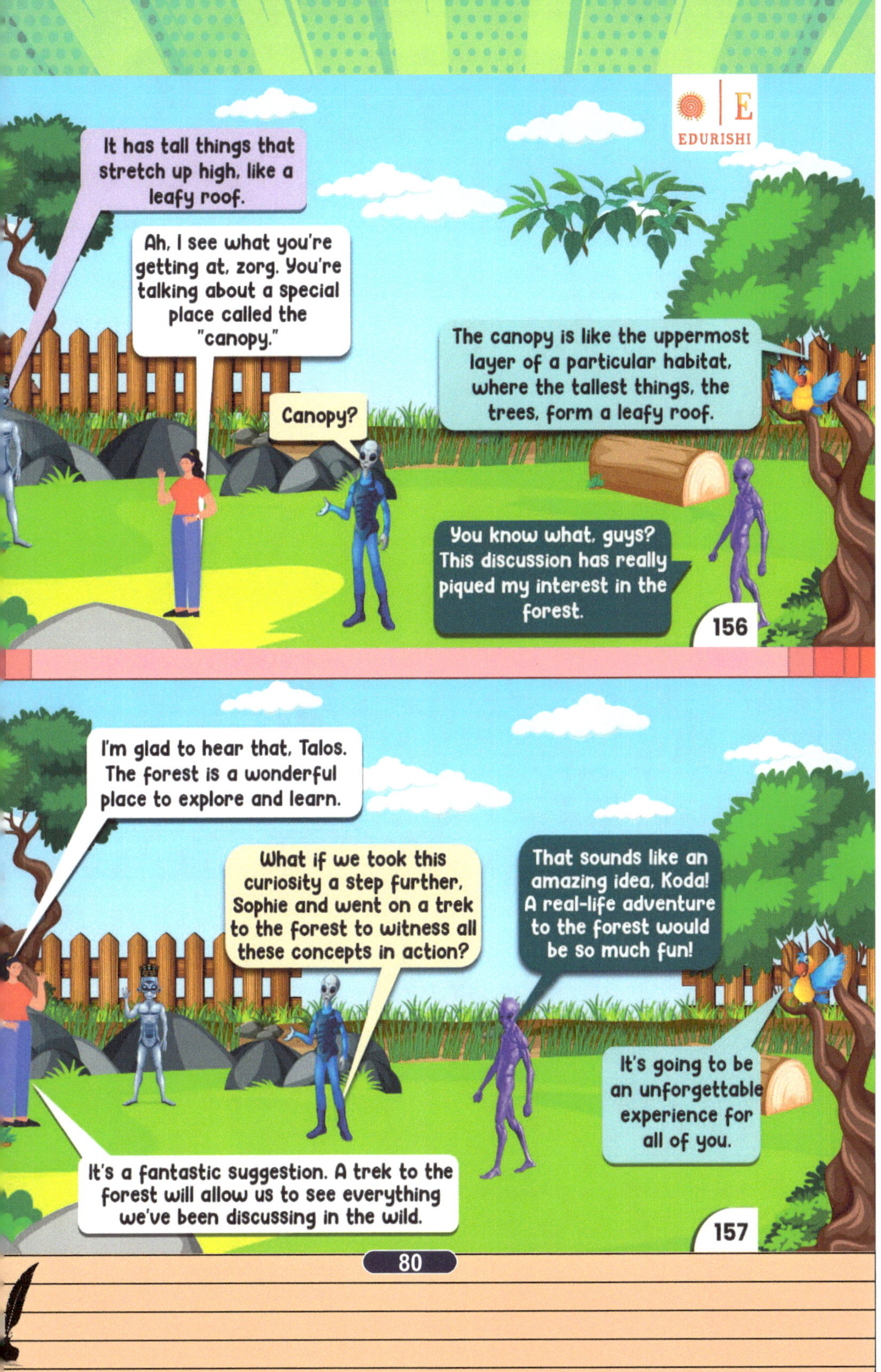
EDURISHI
It has tall things that stretch up high, like a leafy roof.
Ah, I see what you're getting at, zorg. You're talking about a special place called the "canopy."
The canopy is like the uppermost layer of a particular habitat, where the tallest things, the trees, form a leafy roof.
Canopy?
You know what, guys? This discussion has really piqued my interest in the forest.
156
I'm glad to hear that, Talos. The forest is a wonderful place to explore and learn.
What if we took this curiosity a step further, Sophie and went on a trek to the forest to witness all these concepts in action?
That sounds like an amazing idea, Koda! A real-life adventure to the forest would be so much fun!
It's going to be an unforgettable experience for all of you.
It's a fantastic suggestion. A trek to the forest will allow us to see everything we've been discussing in the wild.
157
80

Sophie and her friends, arrived at the edge of the forest, eager to embark on their adventure.
EDURISHI
Here we are, everyone, at the entrance to the forest. Our journey into the world of the forest begins now..
And who's that little companion, Sophie?
Hello everyone I am delighted to be your guide today.
Every one meet Sogar, he is going to be our guide and teach us more about the forest.
158
Look at that! Birds flying up. It's like a whole other world up on the roof.
Exactly Talos. The canopy is like the roof of the forest, formed by the tall trees. Its home to many creatures and provide shed and shelter.
I see a lot of young saplings here. Is this part of the forest's?
Oo-oo! Seeds everywhere!
Yes, it's the part of forest's regeneration.
159
81

Sogar's right! Those seeds are part of the forest's "seed dispersal" mechanism. Creatures like Sogar help spread seeds around, allowing plants to grow in new places.
This is a sign of the forest's ability to bounce back after disturbances like deforestation.
It's like a natural cycle of renewal.
Yes Zorg. It is.
160
As they continued their exploration, they noticed a hillside showing signs of soil erosion.
Look at this, everyone. The soil here seems to be washed away. What's happening?
Yes, Talos. It's a consequence of poor land management. Soil erosion can be a significant issue for the forest.
This is an example of soil erosion.
It's crucial to protect the soil, not just for the forest but also for the ecosystem downstream.
SOIL EROSION
161

Hey, everyone, come take a look at this! There's a hole in the ground.
You've stumbled upon something fascinating, Koda. This is humus.
Humus is the dark, nutrient-rich material that forms when organic matter like leaves, twigs, and plants decompose in the soil.
Humus? What is it?
It's like a natural compost pile.
Nature really has its own way of taking care of itself.
162
Which place is it? It's looking like barren land.
This is so different from the lush forest we've been exploring. Why is there no forest here, Sogar?
It's like a wasteland. What happened?
Guys lets get a closure look of that place first.
163

Unfortunately, what you see here is the result of deforestation.
Deforestation... Sophie told us it's a problem.
Deforestation is when people cut down trees without thinking about the consequences. It disrupts the forest balance.
It's heart breaking to see the impact it has on this place.
DEFORESTATION
164
Look at these tiny creatures breaking down leaves.
Excellent observation, Koda. Those are the "decomposers" we talked about. They play a crucial role in keeping the forest healthy.
You can feel the air here, so fresh. It's like the forest is breathing.
You're absolutely right, Talos. The forest maintains a delicate "balance of oxygen and carbon dioxide," crucial for our planet's well-being.
165
EDURISHI

EDURISHI
As the group, continued their forest exploration, they suddenly felt the first raindrops fall from the sky.
Rain what should we do, Sophie?
I know a place! Follow me to a nearby cave.
We need to find shelter, fast. The rain can make the forest quite wet and cold.
Hurry, everyone! Sogar knows where he's going.
166
Sogar led the group to a nearby cave nestled beneath the trees, providing a dry refuge from the rain.
Thank goodness for this cave, Sogar! We'd have been soaked otherwise.
You're right, Sogar. Rainwater is crucial for the forest's life. It provides water to drink and supports the plants.
But Rainwater is important.
Speaking of water, what else can it be used for?
167
85

As they watched the rain outside, Sogar highlighted the changes in the state of water.
EDURISHI
I remember learning about the different states of water.
Water exists in three states: solid as ice, liquid as water, and gas as vapor. These states change depending on temperature.
Just like Rainwater changes.
You're absolutely right, Sogar. Rainwater starts as vapor in the clouds, condenses into tiny droplets, and falls to the ground as liquid rain. It's a fascinating part of the water cycle.
168
Let me show you the water cycle.
WATER CYCLE
CONDENSATION
EVAPORATION
PRECIPITATION
COLLECTION
169

With the rain outside gradually subsiding, the group, decided to continue their exploration of the forest.
EDURISHI
Wow, nature's magic at work! But what happens when that water falls on land?
It is absorbed by the soil and taken up by plants.
Exactly Sophie! And some water flows into rivers and underground reservoirs, becoming a vital resource for both nature and us.
That's right! It is a continuous movement of water on Earth, from evaporation and condensation to precipitation.
170
But what about floods? I've heard about them.
Floods occur when there's heavy, rainfall, and the land can't absorb water. It can lead to overflowing rivers and causing damage.
So, it's like water covering the land?
That's right, Koda. It can be dangerous and cause damage to homes and ecosystems.
171
87

They move to a different location. They journey to a nearby open field where the landscape is notably different from the forest.
EDURISHI
What happens when there's not enough rain in the forest?
That's right. One of the first things affected is the soil. Less rain means less water getting into the ground.
See this soil we're standing on. When it doesn't get enough rain, it becomes dry and compacted. And it is called as drought.
It's clear how much we rely on water, and how devastating drought can be.
Absolutely, Koda. Every drop counts when it comes to conserving water.
172
Sogar, we can't thank you enough for all the knowledge you've shared with us about the forest and the effects of drought.
You've been an incredible guide, Sogar, and your insights have given us a deeper understanding of this beautiful place.
Thank you all for your kind words.
We'd love to stay longer, but it's time for us to head back to our place.
Ok! Goodbye everyone.
173

After their enlightening forest adventure, they returned to Sophie's house. They were excited to explore the various aspects of water related topics they had encountered in the forest.
Now, let's take our understanding of water to the next level by exploring these topics right here at home.
So water is a lifeline for everyone.
Water is indeed our lifeline. It's essential for drinking, cooking, cleaning, and so much more. Without it, wouldn't be possible.
What happens to the water after we use it?
Lets go to the kitchen to understand this.
174
As they gathered around the kitchen, Sophie filled a glass of water from the faucet to illustrate.
After using the water is goes down the drain. That's where sewage comes into play. Sewage is the used water from our homes and businesses, including everything that goes down our drains and toilets.
So, what do you do with all that sewage water?
We treat it to make it safe for the environment. The filtration process is a crucial step. It removes impurities and harmful substances from the wastewater.
175

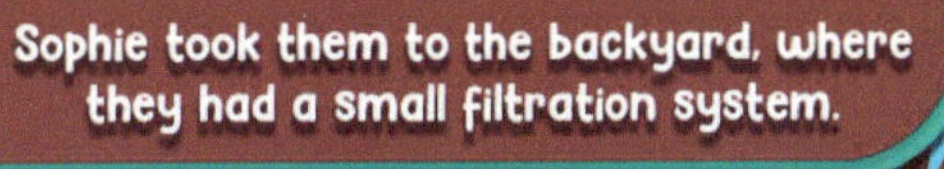

Sophie took them to the backyard, where they had a small filtration system.

EDURISHI

I see, like a mini water treatment plant right here.
Exactly, Zorg. And in larger cities, we have wastewater treatment plants that do this on a much larger scale.
So, it's about keeping our water clean and safe for everyone.
yes, and it's also crucial for sanitation and preventing diseases.
176

Without proper wastewater treatment, contaminated water can lead to health problems.
Are there other ways to manage sewage if we don't have these systems?
Yes, there are alternative arrangements for sewage disposal, like septic tanks or composting toilets.
They work well in areas where centralized systems aren't feasible.
It's crucial that we conserve water to ensure there's enough for everyone and for nature. Every drop counts.
That's absolutely right Talos.
177

As Sophie, Zorg, Talos, and Koda continued their exploration and discussions, they received an unexpected message on their communication device. It was from Onidura, their home planet.

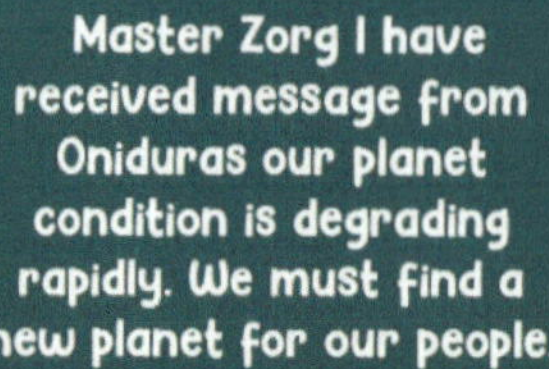

As Sophie, Zorg, Talos, and Koda returned to Onidura, they were met with a disheartening sight. Their once-thriving planet was now suffering from environmental degradation.

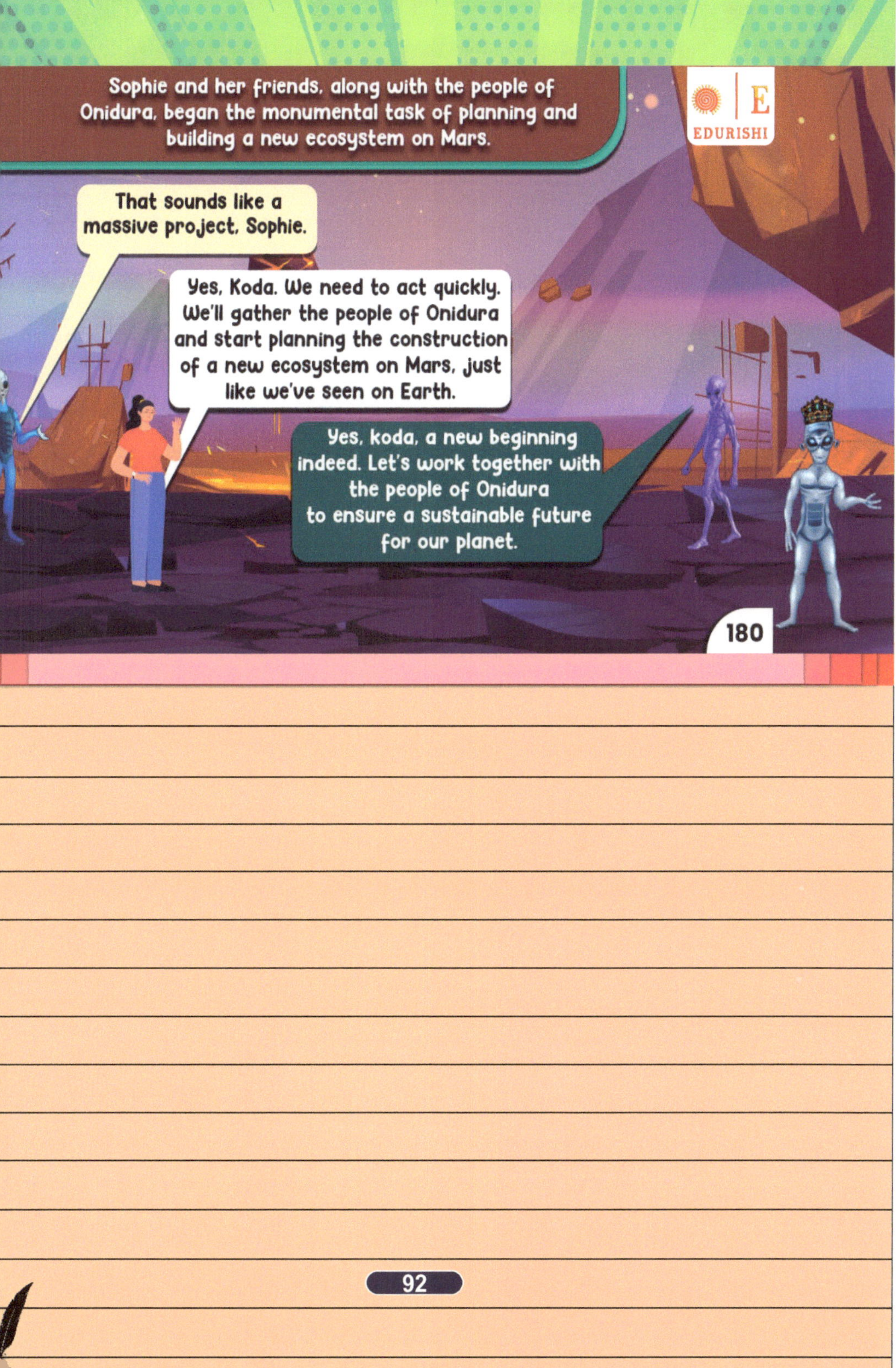

Sophie and her friends, along with the people of Onidura, began the monumental task of planning and building a new ecosystem on Mars.
That sounds like a massive project, Sophie.
Yes, Koda. We need to act quickly. We'll gather the people of Onidura and start planning the construction of a new ecosystem on Mars, just like we've seen on Earth.
Yes, koda, a new beginning indeed. Let's work together with the people of Onidura to ensure a sustainable future for our planet.
EDURISHI
180

What will be the future of Onidurans...?

Will Zorg, Talos and Sophie be able to build a new ecosystem on Mars?

The Adventure continues in the next part...

SUBSCRIBE to EduRishi for more such amazing content!

S.T.E.A.M QUEST

Four Levels of Assessment

- Level 1- Class 4&5
- Level 2- Class 6&7
- Level 3- Class 8&9
- Level 4- Class 10

₹ 200/-
FOR WHOLE YEAR

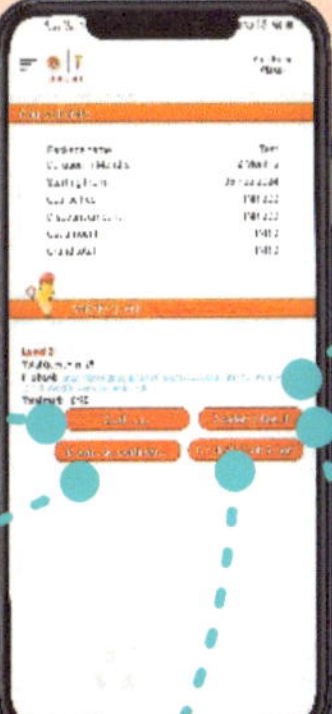

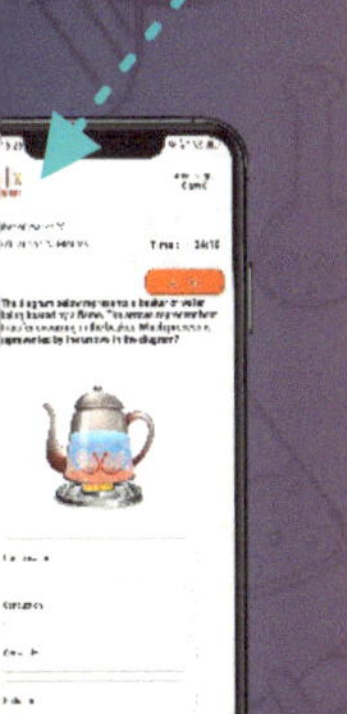

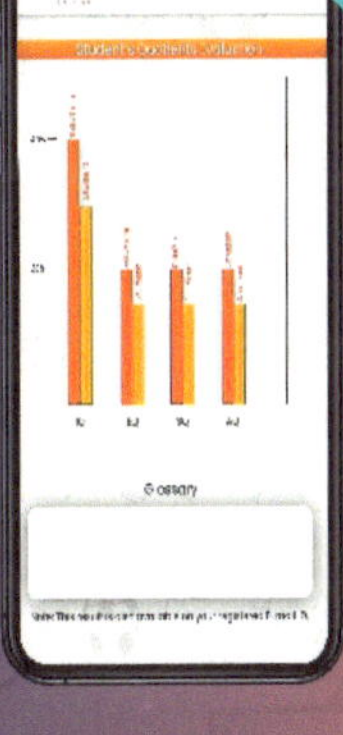

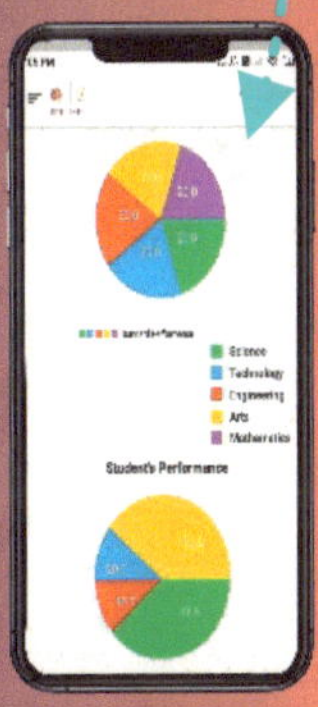

IQ

EQ

AQ

SQ

94

Notes